MW01643581

The HORSE

Longmeadow Press

Longmeadow Press

The HORSE

The comprehensive guide to breeds, riding and management

Pamela Macgregor-Morris &
E. Hartley Edwards

With a foreword by
Anne Moore

Acknowledgments

All the photographs in this book are Orbis copyright with the exception of the following:

Barnabys: 85T, 119 – Jane Burton/Bruce Coleman Ltd: 98/9 – John Burton/Bruce Coleman Ltd: 106/7, 108/9 – Bruce Coleman Ltd: 24/5, 62, 124/5, 142 – Rex Coleman: 68/9, 136/7, 138/9 – Colorific!: 119, 123 – Colour Library International: Title page – Anne Cumbers: 8/9 – Fox photos: 115 – W. L. Hamilton: 95 – Keystone Press Ltd: 136 inset, 137 inset, 138B – E. D. Lacey: 56, 57, 63, 64 inset, 67, 86/7, 128/9, 130, 131, 140, 141 – M. Leigheb: 46T – Erich Lessing/ Magnum: 76/7, 78, 79 – Marka: 103 – T. Micek: 104 – Pony Magazine: 32 – P. Popper: 99 inset, 101 – Peter Roberts: 50/1, 52, 53, 54/5, 60/1, 64/5, 66, 85B, 126 – W. W. Rouch: 89 – J. Six: 102 – Spectrum: 46B – Sport and General: 70, 71 – Tony Stone: 28/9, 30/1, 34/5, 38/9, 42/3, 46/7, 48, 49, 143 – Daily Telegraph: 90, 91 – Sally Anne Thompson: 20, 41 inset, 82/83, 84, 88, 92, 94, 96, 97, 110/111, 112, 117, 118, 120, 121, 124/5 inset, 127 – Tiofoto: 114 – V. Wentzel: 113 – ZEFA/Shostal: 122.

Endpapers: Arts Council of Great Britain

The following writers also contributed to this book: Josephine Hanson and G. W. Serth.

Published by Longmeadow Press
P.O. Box 10218
201 High Ridge Road
Stamford, CT 06904

This edition published in 1987 by Black Cat, an imprint of Macdonald & Co (Publishers) Ltd,
Greater London House, Hampstead Road, London NW1.

ISBN 0-68140364-0

Printed in Italy

Front cover photograph by Tony Stone Associates

Foreword

There cannot be many people who, at some time or another, have not been fascinated by the horse, whether by the pageantry of the Trooping of the Colour, royal weddings and other state occasions, or by the fearless exploits of show jumpers and eventers, or even by the no less intriguing moorland ponies roaming free, or the sadly disappearing patient, milkman's friend.

The horse has always been part of man's heritage. It has carried great kings and emperors into battle, pulled stage coaches and gun carriages, suffered countless skirmishes between cowboy and Indian, and delivered messages and mail which made and sometimes changed the course of history. The horse has always been man's companion, servant and friend. Under man's guiding hand it has impressed us all with its breathtaking speed on the racetrack, its ability to jump seemingly impossible obstacles, its grace and elegance in the dressage arena and its amazing agility and intelligence in Pony Club games and gymkhana events.

Thus it is hardly surprising that the interest in the horse world has escalated by leaps and bounds. Gone are the days when horses were only for the select few who lived in large country houses with stables and acres of land over which to ride. Nowadays, thanks to the work of organizations like the British Horse Society and the Pony Club, almost anyone can enjoy the pleasures of riding at any one of the countless riding schools which have sprung up all over the country.

However, with this enormous interest comes a desire and indeed a necessity for people to learn more about the horse, its origins, the various breeds and types, its uses, how to ride and train it, and perhaps most important, how to care for it. All these facts should be known by everyone who enjoys and appreciates horses, whether they are competing, riding for pleasure or participating from an armchair.

This is where *The Horse* comes into its own: it explains and reveals the horse world in a lively, interesting and informative way. The authoritive and entertaining narrative teamed with the magnificent illustrations gives the reader all the information he or she will ever require to understand this fascinating and majestic animal.

I have thoroughly enjoyed reading this book and hope that many others will have the same pleasure. In fact, *The Horse* is a must for any horse lover.

Contents

Chapter I
Care and Management

Stabling, feeding and grooming your horse

PERHAPS the most important aspect of horse management, which is learned only by experience and yet is so vital to the well-being and consequently the performance of any horse or pony, is the necessity to regard each animal as an individual. Horse management by rule of thumb will sustain life but little more. It is also essential to study the separate and often diverse requirements of every horse; to relate the ratio of work to nourishment with every horse and to remember the old adage that 'the eye of the master maketh the horse fat'.

However, few modern horse owners have any alternative to combining the role of master and man; not many people today can afford the services of a groom. Those who can afford it often have to make do with inadequate and sometimes inexperienced labour. The days of the old-fashioned groom with a small army of strappers at his command have vanished forever. The present-day owner is likely to be his own groom, strapper, stable boy and tack-cleaner and unless he is well versed in all of these skills he is unlikely to enjoy the pleasure to be derived from riding a sound, fit and healthy horse.

To the true horse-lover the necessity for filling all these roles is infinitely rewarding and well worth the effort involved. But as time is probably more precious than ever before, it is essential to dispense with the finer niceties in which the old-fashioned horse-master was able to indulge. One must concentrate instead upon the basic principles to be followed if the best is to be gained from horse ownership, which inevitably involves a high degree of reciprocity. Unless one is prepared to expend effort, energy and hard cash on the maintenance of an animal, it is unreasonable to expect very much in return.

A horse is an animal that is inherently generous but its temperament reflects the treatment which has been meted out to it from its earliest days. If it has been treated kindly but firmly since it was a foal it will respond by giving its utmost in return. If it is chivvied and bullied it will be sullen and resentful. If it is allowed to assert its own will on that of its handler it will lose respect for mankind.

Health and physical fitness are the most important attributes of any horse. Health in the horse at grass is one thing; health in the stabled animal is quite another. The horse that lives at grass, which is after all the natural environment, can survive the period when grass is growing and full of nutriment (from May until August or even September) without extra nutriment, if it is not asked to do any work. But as soon as a horse goes into work it will need more concentrates than nature can supply unaided. As soon as

the grass ceases to contain sufficient nutriment for even basic subsistence, it is essential to make available additional supplies of bulk food such as hay–and hard feed to produce energy in the form of corn.

Extremes at either end of the scale are bad. If a horse is underfed–and in winter it needs food to keep it warm in addition to providing energy for work–it will soon look debilitated and so will be unable to perform adequately those functions for which it has been acquired. If, on the other hand, it is overfed and underworked, and particularly if it is over-indulged in a high protein diet, it will soon become unmanageable and often unsound into the bargain. A surfeit of corn will go to its head and legs simultaneously. Too much corn affects horses as alcohol affects human beings. Over-freshness, which leads to lack of control, is one result and filled legs and various unsoundness of the feet are others.

It is necessary to emphasize the importance of having clean, fresh water available to the horse at all times, whether the animal is at grass or stabled. Horses that are given a constant supply of water to drink rarely fall victim to colic, which is generally reserved for those that are watered at too long intervals and then drink too much, either because they are desperately thirsty or because they have learned, from bitter experience, to stock up to capacity against the long interval which will intervene before they are offered a drink again. So water should be freely available at all times, save only shortly after a long, hard period at work, when a tired and thirsty horse should be allowed to drink only sparingly lest chills and colic ensue.

For horses kept at grass it is only humane to provide companionship and a shed wherein they can shelter from flies in summer and the wet of winter–for horses can stand extreme cold far more easily than protracted periods of rain. Both stabled horses and those kept at grass require, in addition to constant cold water, a hay net or rack that is filled morning and night, and regular and varied feeding of corn, bran and chaff with various additives.

In addition, horses need daily exercise and grooming and a clean bed on which to rest. Ideas are constantly being revised in the horse world. Many of the professional stables, with too few staff and too many horses, have resorted to sawdust or peat-moss as an alternative to the traditional straw bedding. Many amateurs, who tend their animals both in the morning before going off to a day's

Nutritious summer grass alone may not be enough if these horses are made to work

work and again on their return, have opted for the deep-litter system of bedding. This is the system whereby only the droppings are removed and a layer of clean straw put on top. This reduces the mucking-out period but results in a back-breaking job for the lone operator at the end of the winter, when the demands of hygiene indicate that the boxes be completely cleared of a six-month accumulation. Only trial and error will determine which method is best for the hard-pushed owner and his individual horse.

Whichever method is decided upon, it is essential that the horse's hooves be picked out each morning, lest an accumulation of heating manure should cause the dread disease of thrush to develop in the horse's frog. (This is an area in the hoof which is pliable like firm rubber, and which acts as a shock absorber as it is the first part of the foot to touch the ground.) Thrush broadly corresponds to foot-rot in sheep and causes lameness in the victim.

Horses should be fed little and often, and with strict regard to the amount of work they are doing. Foods, such as oats, which produce heat, should be fed in moderation to horses that are not in hard work. Nuts are useful to owners inexperienced in feeding a horse and to those who are trying to combine the smooth running of their stable with a thousand other responsibilities, as most of us are. These nuts include all the necessary vitamins and minerals, and instructions for feeding are usually printed on the bag.

Those who prefer the more traditional feeding methods must be guided by the type of horse (the better bred it is, the better feeding it requires), its age (old horses require more concentrates), and the work it is doing. Three feeds a day are minimal for the hunter in winter and four are better. The amount of corn, which may also vary with the size of the animal, can differ from 10 lb a day for a 16-hand hunter to nearly double that amount for a racehorse of the same size. Some horses can take very little corn indeed and their feeds must be supplemented by such additives as flaked maize, sugar-beet pulp (previously soaked for 24 hours), broad bran (increasingly difficult to obtain) and molassine meal–all designed not only to give nourishment but also variety to the diet.

Grooming is not essential for the animal at grass. Indeed, unless the horse is in work, it is better with the natural oils left in its coat. But it should not be brought home sweating, turned out in the field and then left with the saddle-marks until the following weekend. It should be brought home cool, by walking the last mile or so. It may then be left in its box to dry off and turned out to roll in

reasonable weather. When the animal is dry, the sweat should be removed or your horse will be very uncomfortable.

If stabled, it should be brushed over–cursorily, if time is short–before being exercised, and then well strapped upon its return. After hunting, when the horse is tired, it should be well rugged-up and checked for cuts and bruises which may need attention. Later it should be visited to ensure that it has not broken out in a sweat, for this will lead to a chill. It can then be left until the following morning when the mud will have dried and be easy to brush out, or an electric groomer can be used.

The horse's state of mind during the time when it is in its stable, which may be 22 hours out of 24, is very important. If it is comfortable in its box, that is half the battle. It is equally important for the animal to be able to look out of the box, for this will prevent boredom. If your horse has a friend in the box next door, so much the better. If this is not possible, remember that many famous and successful horses have struck up lasting friendships with animals such as sheep, goats, donkeys, dogs or even cats and bantams. Boredom is the arch-enemy and leads to such habits as weaving (a nervous habit where the horse rocks and sways from side to side), crib-biting and wind-sucking (both of which involve the swallowing of air while arching the neck). Every precaution should be taken to avoid the onset of these stable vices.

It is dangerous to over-simplify the most basic details of horse management, which include regular worming at least

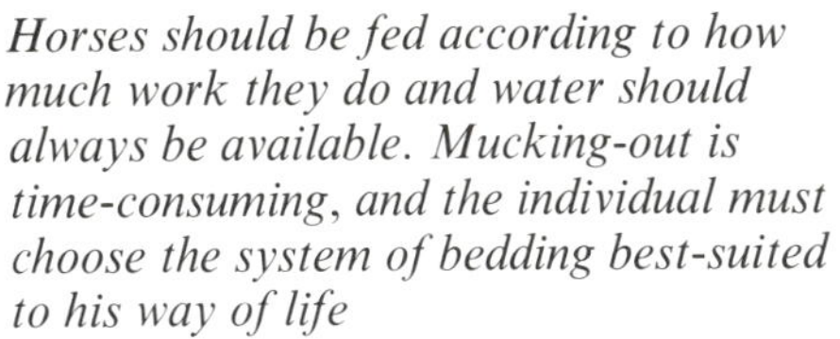

Horses should be fed according to how much work they do and water should always be available. Mucking-out is time-consuming, and the individual must choose the system of bedding best-suited to his way of life

twice a year. The golden rule is always to enlist the services of a really good veterinary surgeon. Establish a working relationship with him and if anything appears to be amiss with the horse, call him at once. Many incipient troubles can be nipped in the bud if they are treated in time, and a veterinary fee is a cheap price to pay for knowledgeable advice. Not only do you owe it to your horse to call in the vet if in doubt, but with the price of horses as high as it is today, you owe it to yourself. Your love and care will certainly be repaid.

Hints on buying a pony or horse

ESSENTIALLY the act of buying a horse is as simple as that involving any other commodity. A horse does not, of course, have a price tag on his ear, and so the settlement of a mutually agreeable figure will be a matter for negotiation between the parties. Once a figure is agreed the procedure is the same as for a bar of soap or a box of chocolates – money changes hands and the goods become the property of the purchaser.

In the case of a bar of soap or a box of chocolates, however, there is little doubt that the articles purchased will be suitable for the purpose required of them by the buyer. But that is not necessarily so when it comes to buying horses and ponies. One horse might be entirely right for one person and completely unsuitable for another. Suitability, therefore, must be the paramount consideration in the mind of the would-be owner, bearing in mind the facilities available for the animal's keep, the personal conformation of the rider, his or her temperament and ability and the purpose to which the horse or pony is to be put.

A novice rider, for instance, may dream of being the centre of an admiring, envious group of friends by cavorting nobly on a dashing Thoroughbred, but if he is wise he will not attempt to turn his dream into reality. The Thoroughbred is indeed the super-horse, the Rolls-Royce of the equine creation but it is usually highly-strung, full of courage and frequently impetuous.

Additionally, the Thoroughbred demands considerable attention, particularly in winter, when it must be stabled, rugged and generally cossetted. There are probably Thoroughbred horses that will winter out in the paddock but they are the exceptions.

The novice rider will usually be happier with a half-bred horse or one with some native pony blood in its breeding. These will not have the speed and scope of the blood horse but they are more likely to possess an equable temperament and be less demanding.

These are the most suitable animals for those unable for one reason or another to stable a horse during the winter. Alternatively, go for one of the larger breeds of native pony, for these are well able to carry an adult as well as being suitable mounts for older children. The Welsh Cob, Highland, Dale and possibly the Connemara or New Forest all make good rides for medium-sized adults and the first three are quite capable of carrying weight out of proportion to their size. All, of course, are infinitely tough, rarely sick or listless and most are possessed of good temperament and an enviable sagacity.

For smaller children there are the Welsh ponies, the Exmoor and Dartmoor and, for the very small, the Shetland. These, or outcrosses from them, are the best sort of all-round pony for a child. Admittedly, the quality, blood-types of pony are lovely, but they require special care and attention and bold, competent riders.

Potential purchasers, would therefore be well advised to spend a little time considering the sort of horse that would fit their individual requirements, rather than making an impulsive decision they may regret. When buying a pony for a child even more thought should be given, particularly with regard to temperament and the child's ability. A young, inexperienced pony, for example, will not suit a similarly inexperienced child, nor will a nervous pony suit a child of the same highly-strung disposition.

Having decided what is wanted, there are then several other factors to be considered, not least of which is the price one is prepared to pay. Basically, price depends on age, conformation, performance and potential and, of course, on the soundness of the horse. Let it be said at once that the purchase of a horse that is unsound or has a history of unsoundness will prove to be an expensive time-consuming operation, however low the initial price.

A very young horse two or three years old, will cost less than a mature one of between seven and ten years – the prime years of a horse. On the other hand, the young horse is likely to prove just as expensive an acquisition by the time it has been kept unused for a year to allow it to grow, and then for another 12 or 18 months during its training.

Similarly, one would not expect to pay large sums for a horse well advanced into its second decade, whose working life would necessarily be limited.

The conformation of a horse, that is its make and shape and general proportions, is an indication of its potential performance. All else being equal, a horse truly

Have the horse run out at walk and trot, and note whether the action is true. Watch for legs that brush one against the other

proportioned and of good conformation should be more efficient and have a longer working life, than one not so adequately cndowed.

It is advisable on these grounds to buy the best physical specimen that one can afford. Bear in mind, however, that since horses are *not* machines, there are many strangely put-together animals that are excellent performers.

The sort of horse that would be placed in the show-ring will, of course, be more expensive, and if that is what is required the purchaser must be prepared to spend much more money. On the other hand, if the buyer does not aspire to showing, taking part in point-to-points or competing at the higher levels of equine sport, a less perfect specimen, while in good health and not displaying any outrageous faults of make and shape, will be more suitable and will cost less money.

Performance must also influence price. The proved eventer, show jumper or experienced gymkhana pony, costs more than the untried animal.

Size is another factor to be considered. In the pony world particularly, animals not falling into the specific height classes of 12.2, 13.2 and 14.2 hh but which possess the attributes of a good pony, will be less expensive.

For instance, the pony that grows a little over 14.2 hh will be excluded from many competitive classes for that reason and yet will be too small to compete with much chance of success in a class for larger horses. Such an animal may nevertheless be a good buy for the person whose interests are not directed towards competition.

Whether to buy a mare or gelding is not a matter to worry too much about, but it should be recognized that some mares can be troublesome when in season – the period when the ovaries are functioning and there is a discharge of mucus from the vulva. This is the time when the mare is sluggish, irritable and given to squealing if her flanks are touched, and she shows a liking for geldings and stallions.

Colour is of even less importance, and it would hardly be sensible to turn down on this count a horse or pony that suited one's requirements in every other respect. None the less a good, strong colour is usually associated with a workmanlike horse whereas weak, wishy-washy colours, particularly in chestnuts, often indicate horses without any great depth of stamina. Chestnut, indeed, is a colour that frequently accompanies a hot temperament and there are people who will avoid it for this reason.

Bearing all these things in mind, how does one set about buying a horse or pony

Tooth decay and other dental defects will affect the action of the bit, so pay attention to the horse's mouth

and what should be looked for when the animal is presented for inspection?

A great many riding horses are sold privately through the sale columns of the equestrian press, in particular those of *Horse and Hound*; others are sold at sales. These latter may vary from small affairs at local markets to established events held regularly at places like Kelso, Hereford and Leicester. In general, sales are not the place for the novice and he would be better advised to buy privately or through a reputable horse-dealer.

Horse-dealers have been much maligned, although dealers of the back-yard type do deserve their bad reputation. But the established dealer is as responsible and honest as any other business-man and usually far more so than his counterpart in the motor trade, for instance. In many cases it is safer to buy from a dealer who has a reputation at stake than from a private person.

A great many private sellers tend to view their geese as swans. They advertise them in suitably glowing terms and, of course, they often have an inflated idea of the animal's value. This is not so in every case, but it is wise when contemplating a private purchase to find out as much about the horse in question as possible before making an expensive journey to see it.

When inspecting a potential purchase, look at it first in its stable, noting its reactions to handling and its general demeanour. It may mean nothing if a horse presents its rear as the door is opened rather than coming forward with ears pricked in greeting but it is indicative of something and is a warning to the buyer to watch his intended purchase carefully. While in the box take the opportunity to pick up all the horse's feet and tap its shoes – a horse that is bad to shoe can be a liability in days when smiths are few and far between and demand exceeds supply.

Now have the horse brought out and take a good look at it, starting with its head. Does it give that desirable impression of kindness, revealed most particularly by the eye? Or is the latter small and pig-like? Even if you are not an experienced judge of a horse, you can tell whether or not its body and limbs are well and pleasingly proportioned. Big, heavy heads, curiously shaped limbs, feet of unequal size, are as obvious to the novice as the expert – it is simply a matter of observation.

For the finer points of conformation, experience and an eye for a horse are necessary and those unsure of themselves on this score had better take along a more expert adviser. Bone, for instance, and general substance is a matter of importance. Bone is measured below the knee, around the cannon, and one would hope to find somewhere near a measurement of eight inches in a horse expected to carry an adult of around 13 stone. The ability to carry weight depends, in fact, upon bone, not upon height or size. Overall, the intending purchase needs to present a symmetrical outline; there should be no meanness in any section of the horse's body.

Have the horse run out at walk and trot and note whether the action is true, straight and economical. Watch for legs that brush one against the other or for feet flung out sideways and brought to the ground in a circular sweep known as 'dishing'. Now let the horse be saddled, again noting its reactions. Let the owner get up first to give a show – the horse should go better for him or her than for anyone else. Afterwards the buyer should ride the animal, taking it away from the stable, into traffic if possible, popping it over a small fence and generally getting the feel of the horse. If, having done so, you find the paces uncomfortable or the horse in some other way unsatisfactory, don't procrastinate – be honest and say it's a nice horse but not the one for you.

Conversely, if you like the horse, and it is important to *like* it since you are proposing to enter into a partnership, buy it *subject to a veterinary examination for soundness* carried out by a veterinary surgeon of your nomination. Do not expect the vet's report to tell you anything about the horse's temperament and behaviour, only about its health.

Lift up the horse's hooves to check whether the animal will be easy to shoe.

To be safeguarded as far as possible, a written description of the horse's qualities and achievements from the seller would be ideal. But this is unlikely to be given, lest too much be read into it and the honest seller be called to account unjustifiably.

None the less, if the buyer either verbally or in writing makes clear his requirements to the seller he has redress under law should he be sold an unsuitable animal. To take an extreme instance, if a man was sold a horse as a good hunter and had stipulated that the horse was to be used for hunting and then found that every time the horse saw hounds it bolted in panic, he would have a case against the seller. The horse, particularly if it could be shown that it had previously behaved in this way, was patently not suited for hunting and the seller did not, therefore, fulfil his side of the bargain.

If you do decide to buy the horse, take the opportunity to find out the diet it is used to so that you can settle it into its new home as quickly as possible.

Remember that nothing perfect exists in the world and that this applies to horses as much as to anything else. Bear in mind the horseman's jingle: 'To his virtues ever kind – to his faults a little blind.'

Horse ailments

ALTHOUGH many horse ailments, especially diseases of the limbs, are avoidable, even with the greatest care from humans, horses may suffer from disease at some period of their lives.

Strangles is a disease often contracted in markets or in transit from Ireland, and the horse will probably show symptoms a few days after purchase. The signs are dullness and refusal to eat, a temperature of 103°F (39.4°C) or more, and a discharge from the nostrils which becomes yellow and sticky. The lymph glands between the jaw bones swell, sometimes to the size of cricket balls or bigger; they are tender and may burst. The nasal discharge hinders respiration so hay is put in a bucket with a teaspoonful of Friar's Balsam, boiling water is poured on and the bucket put into a sack. The horse must be induced to inhale the steam for about ten minutes, twice a day. The abscesses can be made to point and burst by fomenting with hot water, but they may need to be lanced. The nasal discharge and pus from abscesses is highly infectious. Immediate isolation of a suspected case is imperative. Everything which comes in contact with the discharges should be thoroughly cleansed. With good nursing in warm dry surroundings, and plenty of fresh air, the symptoms will subside within a week or so, but the disease strains the constitution and one or two month's convalescence is desirable. In some cases there can be fatal complications.

Tetanus or 'lock-jaw' can be prevented by inoculation. The germ which causes this disease normally inhabits horse dung and wounds fouled by droppings are likely to be infected. Injuries to the feet are especially liable to lead to tetanus. The germ will only grow in the absence of oxygen, thus a large open wound is less likely to be infected than a small punctured one which closes at the surface and traps the germs. Tetanus can be avoided by giving anti-toxin (obtained from the blood of horses which have recovered from the disease) after a recent injury; this gives immediate protection which lasts for one or two weeks. Permanent immunity is conferred by dosing with inactivated tetanus germs which stimulate the horse to produce its own immunity; a course will give protection for life.

Above right: these ponies are recuperating at a convalescent home for horses. One is suffering from an eye complaint, the other from arthritis. The treatment afforded to sick horses varies a great deal from country to country

The symptoms are that the horse's muscles become stiff (often those of the jaw are affected, hence the common name 'lock-jaw'), and the animal cannot open its mouth to eat. Sudden noises cause the horse to go into spasms. The head and neck are outstretched and the nostrils dilated, the third eyelids protrude across the eyes and the patient moves stiffly. The stable should be kept dark and quiet. Tetanus needs prompt treatment by a vet.

Penetrating wounds of the sole of the foot are frequently caused by nails protruding from a loose shoe. Tetanus is always a danger with such wounds. They are treated by paring a hole in the sole around the wound to permit pus to escape, by poulticing and fomenting and, in some cases, by the use of antibiotics. Tetanus is also highly infectious to humans, and has been contracted by those nursing horses thus affected.

Splints are bony growths on the cannon bones, most often of the forelegs. On each side of the main bone is a smaller bone (a splinter bone) of which the upper ends form part of the knee joint. In the young horse these splinter bones are united to the main bone by fibrous tissue which becomes bony with age. Jarring or sudden pressure on the splinter bones before they are united to the main bone will tear some of this fibrous tissue. The area becomes painful and swollen, and later the swelling becomes bony. The pain and lameness disappear, leaving an unsightly lump known as a splint. Most cases recover except for the blemish but if the animal is worked before recovery is complete there may be further damage and prolonged lameness, and finally a much larger splint. Professional treatment in many cases will reduce the size of the ultimate swelling.

Ringbone is a similar complaint, affecting the long and short pastern bones. The membrane covering the bone becomes inflamed and a bony growth appears between the fetlock joint and the coronet. Symptoms are heat and lameness. The horse must be rested but, although electrical treatment has proved effective, complete recovery is rare.

Laminitis is inflammation of the sensitive leaves which join the foot to the horny hoof. Among the causes are overfeeding and a change from poor to rich pasture. Affected animals may lie down and refuse to rise. When they stand they relieve pressure on the toes by putting the forelegs out in front and taking the weight on the heels, the hindlegs being brought forward under the body. The affected feet are hot. The cause should be removed, and forced exercise will improve circulation in the feet and relieve the condition. There are several modern drugs which vets use to treat this disease. Acute cases may become chronic, and lead to permanent incurable lameness and malformation of the foot.

Ringworm is a contagious disease of the skin. Its gravity lies in its ability to spread throughout a stable and to infect men as well as horses. Precise diagnosis is difficult without using a microscope, but any patches of dry scaly skin with broken hairs, especially if circular, should be suspected. Tincture of iodine is a useful first aid application. The disease is spread by contact with an infected animal.

Colic or abdominal pain has numerous causes, of which indigestion is the commonest. Trouble arises when the feeding routine is altered. New hay, green apples, toffees and sweets, large feeds given to tired horses, irregular meal times, and watering after feeding are the most usual causes of colic. Affected animals are in pain, sweat and paw the ground, groan and look round at their flanks, and lie down and roll–which can result in death through a gut being twisted. Sedative

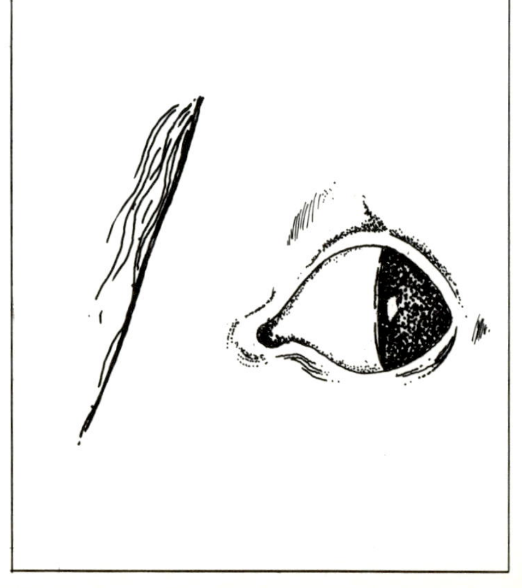

draughts relieve the pain and may prevent the condition getting worse. Neglected cases may become fatal.

A horse's teeth grow throughout its life and are normally kept at proper length by wear against opposing teeth. Uneven wear leads to sharp ridges which cut the cheeks and tongue and interfere with mastication. The horse does not extract full nourishment from its food and so loses weight; uncrushed oats may pass through the intestines and be found in the droppings. It is corrected by rasping the sharp parts with a special file–a painless operation seldom resented by the horse if done with care.

Numerous types of intestinal worms infest horses, the most damage being caused by red worms. Horses grazed on an infested field may ingest so many larvae in a few hours that they never fully recover. Affected horses are thin and have rough coats, and young horses in particular suffer greatly. Severe cases may die. During their progress through the abdomen the worms may invade the blood vessels, and cause irremediable damage. Diagnosis is confirmed by finding the worms or their microscopic eggs in the droppings. Several safe and highly effective proprietary drugs for use against red worms are available. Spread of the disease can be controlled by worming horses before turning them out to pasture, and by daily collection of droppings to keep down contamination of the grass.

Coughing, a symptom of several diseases, is often difficult to control. One disease in which it occurs is influenza, outbreaks of which periodically sweep across the country. Effective preventive vaccines are available and veterinary advice should always be sought.

Broken wind (pulmonary emphysema) is another disease characterized by coughing. In this condition the animal has difficulty in breathing in enough air to oxygenate the blood. Affected horses cough and have a double action of the flanks when breathing out. Mild cases may be kept working by careful management, but they should not be given dusty hay or clover, and more than an hour should always be allowed to elapse after food before working. In some cases of horses suffering from this condition, the symptoms resemble those of hay fever and are successfully treated with drugs. A 'hobdaying' operation (tracheotomy) may be successful if the trouble is in the throat and not the lungs.

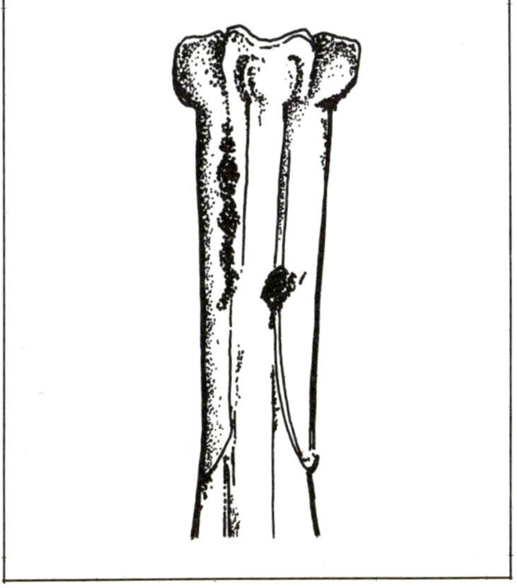

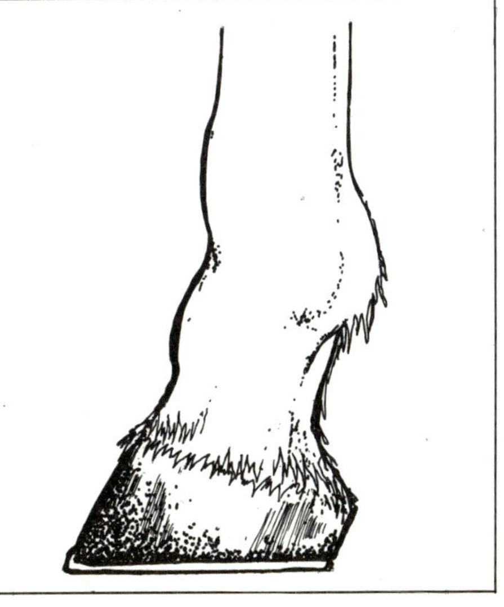

Below, left to right: a painful swelling of the lymph glands denotes strangles; one sign of tetanus is the third eyelid across the eye; splints form on the cannon bones, usually on the forelegs; a ringbone forms on the pasterns

Horse breeding

BREEDING top-class Thoroughbreds for racing, that will fetch £20,000 and above, is a gamble which usually pays off in the long run. Breeding any other type of horse or pony is just as much of a gamble, but there is no guarantee that it will pay. So, pleasant as it might seem to own a stallion and a few mares and to take in a few visiting mares during the three month breeding season in the spring, it is an illusion to envisage one's paddocks knee-deep in lush green grass and buttercups, full of mares and long-legged foals, while simultaneously improving one's bank balance. Horse breeding is definitely not as idyllic as it might appear to the uninitiated.

There are two essential requirements for any stud farm. The first is plenty of land to ensure a good supply of grazing, and this must be accompanied by a knowledge of grassland management. The second is first-class gates and fencing, to ensure that the stock does not get out and that youngsters galloping about the fields run as little chance of injury as possible. Even when every precaution is taken, accidents still happen to young stock.

Given a good stallion and the ideal environment it is quite feasible to make a profit out of stud fees–particularly once your stock has started to make its name in whatever sphere you have chosen to operate, but you will have to do most of the work yourself to be spared paying a crippling wage bill. Breeding from your own mares is a far less profitable proposition. To begin with, very few people wish to buy foals, yearlings or two-year-olds, because of the long waiting period that is involved before these youngsters are of any practical use. Thus one often has to keep them until they are four, break them in and get them going quietly before the customers are interested. By this time, they will have eaten most of the profit, for it is essential to feed young horses properly and advisable to give them shelter during the winter nights.

It is often said in the horse world that 'Only fools breed horses; the wise man lets the other chap do it.' There is always a risk involved, either that the mare may

A Welsh pony in foal. Gestation lasts for 11 months and during this time special attention should be paid to the mare's diet

prove barren, or that she may have difficulty in foaling, or that the youngster may injure itself before it is ready to sell. In no case is there any financial redress, for it is simply the luck of the game.

It must not be forgotten that a stud is rated as an agricultural pursuit, and losses are only allowable against income tax for five years after the stud has been started. If, in spite of this, the intending breeder is still not put off, the very first thing to do is to fence one's land securely. The only safe fencing, and also the most expensive, is made of wooden posts and rails. It is prohibitive in price and has a limited life span, although if it is creosoted or treated with one of the modern improved preparations, possibly tanalized, its durability is greatly improved. Barbed wire fences are most unsuitable and should never be used.

The care of the stallion is very important. Most stallions have a good temperament if they are sensibly handled, but it is as well to remember that they are not geldings; they can be dangerous if they are allowed to think that they are in charge; furthermore, there is no substitute for experience in handling them.

The happier a stallion is, the better-tempered he will be. Some stallions are treated like wild animals and spend most of their lives in a loosebox. There is little wonder that, bored and insufficiently exercised, they roar like lions when they are brought out, spend most of their time on their hind legs and terrify the mares they are meant to cover. If it is not possible to turn them out to grass for a few hours each day, then they must be ridden, lunged or driven in long reins for at least an hour. The more contented they are–and contentment comes from living as normal a life as possible–the more fertile they will be. Neuroticism attacks horses as well as humans, and they will fret and lose condition if they are mismanaged.

Some studs allow their stallion to run with the mares, and certainly in many cases this system works well. But there is always the danger of the stallion getting kicked by a fractious mare, or of a foal being hurt. It is far safer if the stallion serves the mares 'in hand'–that is, on a long rein attached to a bridle, while a helper holds the mare. This, too, can be a hazardous operation. The well-handled stallion who knows his job can look after himself up to a point, and is most unlikely to hurt the handler he knows well, but some mares can be extremely difficult. They kick out both in front and behind, or are so terrified that they are nearly impossible to hold. If they have foaled they are so proud of their offspring that they take no interest whatsoever in anything around them except the foal they have just recently produced.

It is essential to 'try' the mare to see that she is fully in use, or 'in season', before attempting to mate her. If she is forced to receive the stallion's service, perhaps by putting hobbles on her hind legs, she may fight like a wild-cat. In such circumstances she is unlikely to conceive, which renders the whole exercise both highly dangerous and a complete waste of time. A mare can only conceive when the ripe ovum is fertilized by the sperm of the stallion, and if any other time is chosen to suit mere human convenience it will end in disaster.

So it is very important to introduce the mare to the stallion gradually, and only to bring them closer together when she has responded to his advances and, by raising her tail and 'staling', or passing water, indicated that she is both ready and willing to be covered. Mares are usually tried by being introduced to the stallion over a gate, or perhaps at the window of his box, so that they can be led away if they are not ready for mating. Most studs try their own and visiting mares every day. Mares come into season every three weeks during the breeding season. Barren mares have to be watched for the first time, until the oestrous cycle is established; mares with foals have a foaling heat which generally starts on the ninth day after foaling but may occur as early as the fifth day. If the mare does not conceive, she will 'return', or come into season again, three weeks later. Individuals vary very much as to how long they remain in season–some mares are 'on' for only a couple of days, some for a week or more.

If you are a mare owner and wish to breed from her, then you must select a suitable stallion at least three months before the spring breeding season. The various studs operate their own systems concerning expenses, and because one stud has a certain scale of fees there is no guarantee that another stud will operate the same system. You will be well advised to visit a number of studs before deciding which stallion you wish to service your mare. Cost, of course, plays a part in this process of selection. Stallions available are usually advertised in the journals devoted to racing and hunting, notably *Horse and Hound*, *Riding*, *Pony* and the flat-race and steeplechase magazines. When you have made a decision it is up to you to ask the stud owner or his manager to accept your mare for service–reserving a nomination as it is called.

Various expenses are entailed in getting a stallion to service your mare. Obviously you will have to pay for the keep of the mare during the time she is at the stud, and the stud fee which is probably advertised in the journals mentioned. But in addition there will be transport costs in getting to and from the stud, possibly veterinary expenses, possibly farrier's fees, and the usual groom's fee (which is

The male 'teases' the female and if she is ready to be covered she will indicate this by lifting her tail and passing urine

Here the mare is being covered. In season, the mare will come on heat every three weeks until she is successfully mated

usually paid to the stud owner or manager who in turn hands it to the groom). There are other assistants at the stud who contribute to the successful servicing of your mare, and it is a matter of discretion whether you show your appreciation of their work in keeping your mare contented while at the stud. As might be expected, you will have to pay more for your mare's upkeep if she is given extra feeding in addition to being at grass, and if she is stabled at night.

You can be of help to the stud if you let them know something of the temperament of your mare. Tell them if she is, for example, hard to catch; whether she fits in with other horses in the field; and whether she dominates or is easily 'bossed about' by other horses. Also you should mention what veterinary attention she has received recently. Has she had a tetanus toxoid immunisation, for example?

It is sensible to send the mare with the headcollar to which she is accustomed, one which is comfortable and which has worn itself in. Hind shoes are usually removed before the mare departs for the stud; often the stud likes all the shoes to be removed. The stud will see to it that the mare's feet are cared for during the weeks she is at the stud; this of course appears on the bill under farrier's fees.

Mares carry their foals for eleven months, or sometimes a little more. During this time they must be well fed without being allowed to get too fat, or they may have a difficult time in foaling. Pony mares usually foal without much difficulty, and are better left out in the field to get on with the job. Highly bred mares foal in the stable as a general rule, giving the owners and helpers several sleepless nights–for the more valuable the mare, the more important it is to have help at hand in case things go wrong.

Breeding true to type is reasonably certain with registered animals, whose parents on both sides have been recorded back for several generations, though the odd throwback still crops up from time to time. With non-pedigree animals it is not so easy to breed to any set type, and full brothers and sisters may vary in height by as much as two hands.

The type of mare which every stallion owner hopes to have as a visitor is the one who stands calmly and quietly and accepts the stallion. In such cases the mating process takes only a matter of minutes, and the stallion is back in his box soon afterwards and the mare led away to her field, to be served again every other day until she 'goes off'. The mare who bites and kicks is to be avoided at all costs, though few stallion owners are rich enough to request that they be taken elsewhere, despite the risk to their horses.

Persistently difficult mares may be found, when examined by a veterinary surgeon, to have a cystic ovary. Others perhaps are just not meant to breed.

Birth and weaning of foals

BREEDING a foal is all too often a somewhat haphazard arrangement, and results in too many bad animals being bred. It is a great mistake to breed bad horses or ponies. At best, they will end up in a third-rate riding school or trekking centre; at worst, they will travel round the country from market to market and eventually wind up in the abattoir, to finish a pathetic life cycle in a tin of dog meat.

Some foals are bred because people have heard of enormous prices being paid for young horses and ponies, and they want to jump on this lucrative bandwagon. Others are bred because the owner of a favourite old mare, perhaps past work, decides to have a foal–or a series of foals–out of her before she is put down. But very few foals or youngsters make enormous prices, and those that do, command a high figure because of their intrinsic merit and potential, either as show animals or as likely three-day eventers, show jumpers or hunters. Breeding from old or unsound animals is not generally wise, for most unsoundnesses are hereditary and are passed on to the progeny. There is absolutely no point in perpetuating faults of conformation–enough good horses go wrong without adding to the number of those who will not stand up to reasonable work. Besides, a bad animal costs just as much to keep as a good one, so it is in the long run an economy only to breed from the best.

Having satisfied yourself that your mare is, then, fit to breed from, and possessed of good conformation and a sound constitution, it is important to find the best available stallion, not simply the one that lives in the locality and is therefore within easy reach. If possible, he should compliment your mare, so if you have a mare with a straight shoulder, it is imperative to send her to a stallion with good sloping shoulders. If her hind leg leaves something to be desired, look for a stallion with really good hindquarters. Foals have an unfortunate tendency to inherit the worst points of each parent, so it is necessary to minimize these as much as possible.

The size of the stallion will be important, particularly if you are breeding ponies. Unfortunately there is nothing to guarantee that if you send your 12.2 hh mare to a 14.2 hh stallion, she will produce a foal which will grow to 13.2 hh, although, of course, this may happen. One should study the antecedents of the mare and stallion in question to see how true to size they breed. In most cases where a mare has been mated with a stallion considerably larger than herself, the resultant foal, while not disproportionate to her size, will undoubtedly grow up to be larger than her.

The Hunters' Improvement and National Light Horse Breeding Society (8 Market Place, Westerham, Kent) annually makes available to breeders some 70 premium stallions, all of them certified free of hereditary disease and unsoundness, and all Thoroughbreds with a racing record, which members of the Society may use on their mares for a nominal fee. These sires are dispersed throughout the country, and for those who want to breed a good horse without paying a small fortune in stud fees, they are an excellent proposition.

The membership fee for the Society is £3.00 a year, and members pay a stud fee for premium stallions of £20.00. (The fee to non-members is £35.) Each premium stallion is allotted to a particular area, which it tours from April to July and is available at pre-selected centres. Premiums are awarded to stallions at the Annual Stallion Show held by the Society and are worth £500, which enables the owner to offer his horse at such a low stud fee. The Society also runs a National Hunter Show in June for young stock and brood mares, and it maintains its own Hunter Stud Book.

First, however, one must ensure that one has the facilities for breeding a foal, and then rearing it. Adequate, safe grazing is essential, and so is a loose box in which to house the mother and foal during inclement weather. No young animal can benefit from standing under a hedge in the rain all night, or from lying down to sleep in the mud. Two fields are better than one, so that one may be rested while the other is grazed, and they must be safe for a flighty young foal to play in without injury from barbed wire, tins, broken bottles, and other waste products of urban or suburban society. Also check that the hedges do not contain any poisonous plants, such as yew or laburnum.

The stable accommodation must also be checked to make sure it is suitable. If the mare is to foal in the loose box, it should be a very large one. Make sure that there are no sharp protrusions in the

Foals grow very quickly, and soon become independent; a new-born foal will be on its feet and sucking milk within an hour

Breeding from sound parents will be more likely to produce good offspring, like this Arab foal

box, such as nails or wood splinters.

If all the environmental conditions are right and one can thus be satisfied that the foal will be of as good quality as possible, and given the best possible start in life, the gamble is worth taking. It must be realized, however, that breeding a foal is a costly business. A lot of things can go wrong despite expert management. The mare will require liberal supplementary feeding and so, when it is a few weeks old, will the foal. Small native ponies can rear their foals on good grass alone, during the months from May to August, but anything bigger and with more quality will require protein foods such as oats, bran, and flaked maize, not to mention a constant supply of hay while in the stable. It is a good idea to give the mare boiled linseed once or twice a week. To prepare linseed for feeding, allow 2 oz of linseed to 1 pint of water. This should be brought to the boil, stirring continuously, and then it should be simmered for a minimum of four hours. It is most important that linseed is thoroughly cooked before it is fed. When cooked, the mixture will be in a very liquid state, but it turns to jelly as it cools. Half to one pint of the mixture should then be added to a bran mash. It is extremely nutritious, and ensures regular bowel movements.

The mare visits the stallion in the spring, and the gestation period is eleven months, give or take a few days (or sometimes a few weeks). It is a good plan to have a pregnancy test done once the mare has given signs of holding to the service, that is, if she has not come into season again three or six weeks after the mating has taken place. If it is negative, the veterinary surgeon should examine her before she returns to the stud. If positive, her work should be cut down or ceased altogether, and regular morning and evening feeds should be given to ensure that the foal which is growing within her has the necessary access to nourishing food that will do so much to ensure a strong and healthy youngster being born the following spring. Brood mares can do light work, without galloping or jumping, until their pregnancy is quite well advanced, but they should never be pushed to do more than they feel inclined. Light work keeps them fit and sufficient exercise is essential to their well-being, to keep their muscles toned up. If the going is deep or slippery only very slow work is indicated, lest they slip or strain themselves, and it should cease altogether some three months before the foal is due. Do not put the mare out to graze with a colt or gelding as their attentions may cause the mare to 'slip' or miscarry her foal. If she will not stay out happily by herself, it is better to keep her with another mare.

Attention should be paid to the feet of pregnant mares as, with the advance of pregnancy, great strain is placed on the mare's legs. The blacksmith should be called in to attend to them once a month. The mare's teeth should also be examined to ensure she is getting the full value out of her food.

Some mares are very deceptive as to the imminence of foaling. Some will start to form an udder some weeks in advance, with others it is only days, and some will show very little udder at all before the birth. The surest sign is the formation of wax on the teats. When the wax falls off, the mare should be kept under constant observation, for she may foal at any time. When the muscles on either side of the croup – the last stretch of backbone on the rump – fall in, things are beginning to happen.

If all is well, a mare will foal very quickly. If she is let out of her loose box into the field in the morning, she may well have dropped her foal by lunchtime, with no one any the wiser. Lest this should happen the field must be one without a pond, or a river running through it. Mares are very apt to foal into a hollow, and if this hollow is wet, the foal can be drowned at birth.

Providing that the foal is the right way round and there are no complications, the chances are that it will be born, released from its sack, licked clean by its mother, and that it will be on its feet sucking the first colostrum which precedes its mother's milk before its owner sees it at all. But every two hours is none too often to go and look at the mare, while valuable Thoroughbred mares are watched night and day, either from an observation post outside the foaling box or, in the big studs, on closed circuit television.

During foaling the first thing to emerge is the water bag in which the foal is contained. Then the forefeet will emerge, one slightly in front of the other. The nose, resting on the forelegs, appears next and then the rest of the foal is born. Once the shoulders are through, the rest of the body and the hindlegs follow quite easily. Shortly after delivery the foal struggles and breaks the water bag to take its first natural breaths. During the foal's struggles to rise the umbilical cord will be severed. Cotton wool, impregnated with iodine, should be applied to the stump of umbilical cord and the area dusted with antibiotic powder.

If the mare seems to be straining for a long time, and looks distressed, the vet must be called at once. The novice owner can provide little in the way of useful assistance, and may well cause more harm than good. Hints for assisting at a difficult birth are thus out of place here. If the vet knows that the foal is nearly on its way, he will arrange to let his client know where he can be contacted at short notice. Even if the birth has taken place and all appears to be normal, it is highly advisable to have him come and look over the mare and foal to ensure that all is well and that the mare has cleansed, or rid herself of the afterbirth, which is highly toxic if retained.

If the day after the birth is warm and sunny, the mare and foal may be turned out to grass for a couple of hours. The grass will help the mare's supply of milk, which will also be assisted to flow by warm bran mashes, both immediately after the birth and at frequent intervals following. Needless to say, a supply of clean water should also be available.

Foals grow very quickly, and even a new-born foal is surprisingly strong. It is advisable to put a headcollar on it during its first week of life, and to accustom it to being handled and led about. If it should become ill it is then easy to treat, whereas a wild foal is exceedingly difficult. It is never too early to teach a young foal, by kindness and firmness, that it must obey human beings. These early lessons are invaluable as they inculcate a respect for man, but never fear of him.

Feed the mare in a large bowl which will also accommodate the foal's head, for it will very quickly develop a taste for hard food and it will thrive all the better for sharing its dam's feed. As the weeks and months go by it will develop a spirit of independence, and roam further and further away from its mother, who will eventually cease to worry when it is beyond nuzzling distance. Then, at the age of five months or so, the time will come for the foal, now able to graze and feed itself, to be weaned.

The best and kindest way to wean a foal is to lead it into a box, shut the door to prevent the mare following, and then to take her right away and put her into a separate box or with a companion in a field, and if possible out of earshot of her foal. If you have two foals, so much the better. If not, an old pony of good temperament will make a companion for the foal when the time comes to turn it out by day again.

For two weeks it should remain in its loose box, so that by the time it is allowed out it will have ceased to grieve for its mother and will not injure itself by galloping about and trying to find her. For the first few days of the enforced separation, the air will be rent with its cries, and those of its dam, and the owner will just have to harden his heart and remind himself that it has all been done for the best. Gradually the whinneys will become less frantic, until they subside altogether. The foal will take an interest in its food, will be drinking from the bucket of fresh water that is always with it, and the process of weaning will be complete.

Every foal should be stabled at night during the first winter of its life, and fed liberally, with two hard feeds a day and hay ad lib. Foals make their greatest growth during their first year. They can, if necessary, spend their second winter out at night, though many breeders prefer to keep them in. If there is space available this is a better policy, and more conducive to a good night's sleep for the owner, than if he is envisaging his fine youngster subjected to rain and cold, striving to find shelter in an open field.

After weaning, the mare should be kept fairly short of water for a few days, and given a dose of Epsom salts to help her milk to dry up. It is important to keep a watchful eye on her udder, and if it becomes very distended it is best to seek veterinary advice. Most mares will dry off naturally and is unusual that it should cause any trouble.

If it is warm, the mare and foal may be put to grass, both to help the mare's milk supply and to let the foal enjoy the sun

Chapter II
Training of Horse and Rider

Horse control: the seat

THE seat of the rider on a horse is the most important and significant feature of the art of equitation, for from the position of the rider stems everything else: balance, grip, and control.

Although there are variations on the basic seat (for specialist purposes such as dressage, show jumping, steeplechasing and flat-racing, and the straight-legged seat of the cowboy, who rides in a special saddle with very long stirrups), the essentials remain the same. The variations are imposed by different types of saddle, by the style dictated by the instructor, by the make and shape of the individual rider and by the purpose for which the horse is going to be used.

Perhaps the most important thing about any rider's seat is that it should be completely independent of the hands. This is to say that, given a horse that is sufficiently quiet, the rider should be able to knot the reins on its neck in order to prevent them trailing on the ground and then ride down a line of small fences, such as cavaletti, with his arms folded across his chest or held above his head.

The reins are to control the horse; they are *not* intended to be a lifeline for the rider. Those who do maintain or assist their balance by means of the reins will–after inflicting a considerable degree of pain and discomfort on the bars of the horse's mouth–destroy its sensitivity altogether. The rider should maintain his position in the saddle by a subtle combination of balance and grip of the upper leg, down to the knee. In time, when the muscles are attuned to sitting in the right position on a horse's back, the grip soon becomes automatic. Most horsemen, indeed, ride mainly by balance and apply a strong grip only in cases of emergency–when a horse shies at a strange object in the hedge or bucks from over-freshness.

The rider's position on the horse should above all things be a natural one and should be exactly the same with a saddle as without. The correct place to sit is right in the middle of the horse, behind the withers and directly above its centre of gravity, or its balance and equilibrium will be upset. A horse with good shoulders tends to put its rider in the correct position, immediately behind them, and a well-made saddle is designed to make a rider sit correctly, well down in its deepest part. A few riders sit too far forward, or tend to lean forward too much when the horse moves, thus putting themselves in front of their horse's centre of gravity and unbalancing it. But a worse fault is to sit too far back, so that the rider's weight is not only behind the horse's centre of gravity (and so is not evenly distributed over that portion of the horse's anatomy which is designed to carry weight), but is actually deployed over the horse's loins.

The position of the rider should be completely relaxed, though this does not imply that he should effect a slouching position. The back should be straight without being rigid. A stiff back results in tension, which will extend to every part of the rider's body and in turn communicate itself to the horse. The legs should hang down naturally, with the lower leg drawn slightly back so that, looking down at one's knees, one should just be able to see the toes of one's boots projecting below them. The heel should be kept well down at all times so that, combined with the knee, it can act effectively as a shock-absorber. The knee and ankle joints must be flexible to ensure the smoothness of all the rider's movements. A well-sunk heel will assist in keeping the knee close to the saddle and will therefore develop the grip that is essential for security.

The old-time cavalry instructors were very keen on making their recruits do their mounted drill without a saddle but the more recent school of thought considers that bareback riding encourages the novice to make the bad mistake of gripping with the calves, rather than the thighs and that the better method is to encourage riders to quit their irons and ride on a saddle without stirrups, by crossing the leathers in front of the saddle.

An insecure seat and a rider who rolls about in the saddle is very apt to give a horse a sore back–particularly an unfit animal. Sore backs put horses out of work for considerable periods of time.

A rider who sits correctly will have his lower leg free to apply the 'aids' which tell the horse what is required of him. The rider's legs control the horse's hind-quarters and combine with the seat and the back to create impulsion and send it forward, while controlling the direction of the movement. Though the hands are required to exert control, the legs are of greater importance in keeping the horse balanced. Ideally, the horse is balanced between the rider's hand and leg, with the legs creating the movement and the hands containing it.

When jumping fences, the rider's position is even more important than it is on the flat. A rider who gets 'left behind' over an obstacle not only unbalances his

The way that a horse walks can often be an indication of its general performance. The trot (inset) reveals a great deal about a horse's soundness.

and sink his seatbones into the saddle, while at the same time closing his legs against the horse's sides and resisting with his hands to bring the horse back to the required pace in an even and balanced way.

Until a rider is experienced enough to wish to specialize in any one branch of equestrianism he should cultivate a 'general purpose seat', which will suffice to cover any contingency. Above all, harmony of balance and movement is the main consideration of every rider; those who, when looking at photographs of famous show jumpers, criticize details of position, should remember that if the photograph had been taken a second later, it would have looked different. Since riding is a succession of fluid movements, the static movement shown never actually existed. The particular details of a person's seat on a horse vary from person to person; a successful rider, whose aim is to win major competitions, uses position as a means to winning; not as an end in itself. If the rider is comfortable, it goes without saying that the horse will be comfortable too, in which case he will be responsive and co-operative.

The rider's legs should hang naturally, with the lower leg drawn back slightly (left). The forward seat is used when jumping (below and bottom). The closer the rider is to the horse's centre of gravity, the better the horse's balance

horse and causes it to drop its hind legs, which will result in a fall over a fixed or solid fence, but he can also give it a severe jolt in the mouth. A horse very soon comes to expect to be hurt when he jumps a fence and there is no surer way to put him off jumping and start him refusing when he is faced with a fence.

The 'forward seat' is now universally adopted by show jumping riders and, indeed, by any one who jumps a fence, be it in the hunting field, on the racecourse or in the show ring. It was first used and demonstrated between the two World Wars by an Italian cavalry officer, Federico Caprilli. It is perhaps the most revolutionary change in equestrianism that has occurred during the twentieth century.

Up until that time, riders leant forward on taking off over a fence and sat back on landing, as a few of the older hunting people do today and as a steeplechase jockey does on touching down over a big drop (for instance the Grand National's Becher's Brook). But the majority of riders have adopted the forward seat, even when coming down the precipitous slope of the 10 ft 6 in bank in the British Jumping Derby at Hickstead. Caprilli's critics insisted that to sit forward would unbalance the horse and could cause him to crumple up on landing, or at least to peck (stumble) badly. Caprilli argued, quite rightly as was proved in the light of events, that the closer a rider remained to the horse's centre of gravity – that is, poised over his withers – the more likely the horse would be to retain his balance and, consequently, his footing.

The seat of many of the world's most successful dressage riders, in particular those of the German School, is characterized by what is known as 'pelvic push'. It derives from what some consider to be an exaggerated use of the rider's seat bones to push the horse forward. It is an exceedingly ugly seat but an effective one when properly used, though the novice rider need not concern himself with it.

In order to 'go with' the horse it is necessary to lean forward in the faster movements. A hunter showman will sit down even when galloping a horse full pelt around the show ring. But that same man will raise his seat from the saddle, put his weight on to the ball of his foot (thus transferring it from the saddle to the stirrup iron) and stand in his irons when galloping across country behind hounds. It would be very tiring for the horse if he were to sit down to gallop and if the horse were to stumble over rough ground it would not be easy to retain his seat.

Conversely, in order to bring back a horse from a gallop to a slower pace it is necessary for the rider to brace his back

The General Purpose Seat

Seat

A good seat is dependent upon a judicious combination of balance, suppleness and grip of the upper leg, down to the knee. In fact, most horsemen ride mainly by balance and apply a strong grip only in an emergency. The rider's position on the horse should be a natural one. The seat should be well down in the centre and lowest part of the saddle, the shoulders square with the horse's shoulders. The upper part of the body should be upright and show no sign of stiffness. The head should be erect and the rider should look directly in front, between the horse's ears. The back should be straight without being stiff and relaxed without appearing to slump.

Knee and thigh

The knee and thigh should be close to the saddle at all times with the large thigh muscles behind, so they do not lie between the saddle and thigh bone.

Lower leg

The lower part of the leg should be kept back, hanging lightly against the horse's side, close behind the girth.

Feet

The stirrup should rest on the ball of the foot. The heel should be lower than the level of the toes and the ankle joints should be supple enough to flex slightly with the movement of the horse. The toes should point forwards.

Arms

The arms should hang down naturally to the elbows, which should be lightly touching the rider's sides.

Hands

The hands with thumbs uppermost, should be held just above and in front of the front arch of the saddle. Wrists and fingers should be supple. Wrists must not be rounded.

Horse control: hands, legs and feet

IT is essential for a rider to be able to use his hands on the reins in a light and responsive manner, and though this ability can be acquired by experience, good hands are a natural gift. Their possessor is to be envied above all others, for he will be able to settle a restless, fractious, high-spirited horse and make it go freely and kindly. He will exert control so tactfully that the horse does not resent it. On the other hand, the same horse will be driven nearly mad by the constant pain and frustration caused by severe and unsympathetic hands, when a heavy-handed rider attempts to curb its impetuosity.

The secret of good hands is in the principle of give and take, and the cultivation of good hands must be based upon it. When the horse relaxes its jaw and accepts the bit, obeying the restraining action of the hands, the rider gives too and relaxes the pressure on the reins. The balance is so finely adjusted as to be almost imperceptible to the onlooker. Only the feeling which a rider acquires by experience can inform him whether or not he is succeeding in striking this balance, which varies with each horse according to the sensitivity of its mouth, the standard of training attained, the degree of impetuosity in each individual animal and, not least, the circumstances at that particular moment. More effort will be required to control a young horse at the start of a day's hunting, when it is excited by the presence of other horses and the baying of the hounds, than on a solitary morning canter.

Exhibitors often experience considerable difficulty when showing a young horse under a judge whose touch is not, perhaps, as light as their own. Some counteract it by letting the curb chain on the double bridle out a couple of links before the judge gets up. Others encase the curb chain in a chamois leather cover. Even so, they still suffer a great deal as they stand pivoting on their heels, following the progress round the ring of their 'ewe lamb' with increasing horror. Some maintain that it takes a month or more to undo the damage which has been inflicted in a matter of minutes by a heavy-handed, insensitive judge.

Conversely, there are other judges who ride a horse far better than its owner and for whom every horse goes kindly. These are the people who are in demand at all the major shows and whom exhibitors will follow from one end of the country to the other, for this reason.

The well-ridden horse is balanced between the rider's hand and leg. The pressure of the legs behind the girth produces the movement from the hind legs (which are the propelling force), and the hands control this movement. The leg aids are very important and a horse that does not respond and go away from the leg is an infuriating ride. These aids, in which both legs are used evenly to gather up the horse and send it on, or individually to exert pressure for changing direction, are essential for maintaining a balanced and controlled horse.

Reining back also involves a correct balance being struck between hand and leg, with the legs maintaining impulsion and keeping the horse straight, and the hands directing this impulsion into reversing the horse. This is a movement which demands extreme tact and delicacy.

Leg aids are also, of course, absolutely vital to keep the horse straight, to induce work on two tracks in school work and to jump fences. Riders who do not use their legs—and many do not or, if they do, often use them incorrectly—are quite incapable of collecting or balancing a horse, which consequently will move with its nose poked forward, its hind legs trailing behind it and will be completely unbalanced. In this state it is very prone to falls and when a rider is said to have let a horse fall down on the road it is almost invariably for this very reason. The horse has been allowed to move at a slovenly pace, and if it slips it is quite unable to adjust its balance in time to save itself.

The rider's feet play a more passive part, in that they are usually reserved for the reinforcement of the leg aids. They are not a subtle adjunct to leg pressure, but they are often very useful on a half-schooled or obstinate horse which requires a stronger aid to help it to make up its mind to jump a fence or to pass a tractor or bus that it may encounter during the course of its daily exercise. But a rider who indulges in a persistent drumming on his horse's sides, as some less experienced riders do, will soon deaden the sensitivity of the horse's sides, and it will eventually become impervious and unresponsive to this constant irritation. Accepting it as an inevitable and uncomfortable fact of life, it will conclude that it is all quite meaningless and that the best form of defence is to ignore it. This should never be allowed to happen, as once a horse becomes unresponsive to leg aids, it is very difficult to reschool it and the horse will always lack impulsion.

The chief function of the rider's feet is to help him, by means of the stirrup irons, to maintain a correct position in the saddle, from which all else must stem. If the feet are in the right place, with the irons on the ball of the foot and not jammed back into the heel of the boot, and the feet as nearly parallel to the horse's sides as is comfortable, with the heels well sunk, the ankle will form a pivot and a shock-absorber. However, although the ultimate in control will not be achieved without stirrup irons, it is perfectly possible to control a quiet and well-schooled horse without any irons or leathers, which serves to emphasize the importance of the rider's natural balance, independent seat and effective legs.

Indeed, many riders who have been wounded during their Army careers have been enabled, by the use of artificial limbs, to continue their sport at every level, even in the hunting field where they encounter all manner of unpredictable obstacles and situations.

It is said, and not without reason, that women generally have better hands than men, and that women who ride side-saddle have the best hands of all. This is probably true and it relates to the original premise, which is that good hands cannot be acquired without an independent seat. The seat on a side-saddle is the strongest that can possibly be achieved.

Indeed, with her right leg hooked firmly round the pommel, it is virtually impossible to shift a woman riding side-saddle, no matter how much the horse may buck, nor how swiftly it may leap to one side shying at some real or – more often – imagined horror which assumes excessive proportions when it is over-fed and under-exercised. The only real danger to a side-saddle rider is if the horse falls. If it falls on its offside, all is well and she is thrown clear. If it falls on the near-side, she may be trapped beneath it.

But at all events, she never needs to hold on by the reins, so her hands are able to perform their correct function, which is to guide and to control. The reins are never a lifeline, so with a strong and secure seat the side-saddle rider is able to exert a contact that is as light as is compatible with control. By the same token, one could argue that legs are also superfluous in the control of the horse. The side-saddle rider is restricted to one, and a stick has to fulfil the function of the other. But this very fact is sufficient to deter many people from cultivating the considerable art of side-saddle riding. They feel, rightly or wrongly, that after a lifetime spent in riding astride they would 'miss their other leg'.

In the end, nevertheless, the art of riding always comes back to hands, and they in turn depend to a very large extent upon confidence. A rider who has lost, or is in the process of losing, his nerve, starts to snatch and to clutch when things go wrong. His fear is communicated to the horse and then trouble starts. Courage remains at the root of all things which pertain to dealing with the horse, for a relaxed rider produces a generous and co-operative horse.

Facing page: a young rider embarks on her first lesson in horse control. Below: opening gates while on horseback requires firm but sympathetic control with the legs

Horse movement: walk and trot

A GOOD horse is almost invariably a good walker, and every judge of a horse will greatly value one which walks alertly with a long, swinging stride that covers the ground well, giving an impression of courage, an interest in its surroundings and of free forward movement.

The horse's shoulders, which govern movement at all paces, should swing freely in both walk and trot, and, indeed, in the faster paces. Set-back, sloping shoulders will produce a long and swinging stride. Straight, upright shoulders sometimes hardly seem to move at all, while movement that comes only from the knee will produce a short and choppy stride, tiring both for mount and rider, and very uncomfortable. It is usually a sign of underbreeding, and common horses, though they may be admirably suited to the requirements of novice riders in riding schools, are never the choice of an experienced horseman, who requires quality and courage above all else.

The foot should be picked up and put down again without shuffling or hesitation. Whether it be an ordinary, extended, free or collected walk, it is a slow pace of four-time on disassociated diagonals. If it begins on the off-fore, the order of footfalls following is: near-hind, near-fore, off-hind, then off-fore again.

The trot is a very important pace for many reasons. It is a pace which reveals a great deal more about a horse's action and soundness, than can ever be ascertained from the walk or from the canter or gallop. It reveals whether the horse moves straight or throws its feet outwards, an action known as dishing, or inwards, which is called plaiting and is by far the worse of the two extremes, as it is possible for the horse to trip itself up and fall.

The trot will also show whether the horse's legs move too closely together, thus interfering with its own action by knocking its fetlock joints. This is known as 'brushing', and to counteract it the horse should be shod with a special shoe. In extreme cases a leather brushing-boot can be fitted over the fetlock joints. When viewed from the rear, the trot will also indicate whether the horse goes too wide or too close behind. When viewed from the side, it is possible to ascertain whether it swings rhythmically and freely from the shoulder and whether it puts its toe out and covers the ground.

When examining horses for soundness, it is essential to see the horse trotting. A lame horse does not trot evenly. If the lameness is only slight it is often easier to hear than to see. If the animal is trotting along the road, any irregularity of movement can be heard at once. If the horse is really lame, not only will it be visible in the movement of the legs, but the horse will drop its head as it lands on the lame leg.

The trot, then, is a pace in which the legs move alternately on two diagonals, and is a pace in two-time. The right diagonal movement consists of the off-fore and the near-hind, and the left diagonal is the near-fore and the off-hind, with a short period of suspension between them. The ordinary trot, collected trot and extended trot are the three variants of this pace. There is also, though it need not concern us here except as a caution, the 'butcher-boy trot', derived from the delivery boy of many years ago, who would race his pony down the road in order to ensure that the meat arrived in time for lunch. All good horsemen abstain from using this pace. Not only is it extremely uncomfortable for the rider but it is very bad for the horse's legs.

A sitting trot enables the rider to assume a very close contact with his horse, and therefore to exert more precise control over its movements. It is more comfortable in the collected than in the extended paces, and varies in the degree of comfort with the type of action of the individual animal. Some horses are a great deal more 'choppy' than others. A horse with very strong hock action always tends to throw the rider about.

When 'rising' to the trot the rider moves slightly out of the saddle on one beat of the pace and gently down again on the second. This should be a smooth, effortless movement. A rider is said to be riding on the right diagonal when his seat returns to the saddle as the horse's off-fore and near-hind come to the ground. To change the diagonal, the rider should sit down in the saddle for an extra beat before beginning to rise again. The preference of the individual horse, particularly those who are not highly schooled, to be ridden

The trot is a pace that reveals much about the horse's action and soundness, and shows whether it moves straight or whether it throws its feet outwards or inwards

Above: for the relaxed pace of the walk, the rider should sit well down in the centre of the saddle with her back straight, head up, knees and thighs pressed against the saddle, and heels slightly lower than her toes which point forwards

on a certain diagonal may be likened to right or left-handedness in a human. The horse is likely to be more comfortable on one than the other and so is his rider. Most horses prefer to be ridden on the left diagonal, and some will employ all sorts of ruses, such as shying or cantering for a stride or two, in order to shift the rider onto the other diagonal if he insists upon riding on the one which the horse dislikes. The schooled horse should go equally happily on either and this can only be achieved by riding on the diagonal which it does not like, and by constantly changing the diagonals until the horse is equally proficient on either.

The trot is a pace which is employed a great deal. Apart from the walk, it is the only one that is either practicable or safe when riding along the road. Anything faster is not only highly dangerous in traffic, but is also extremely bad for a horse's legs and feet, again because of the jarring to which they are subjected on the surface of a hard, and often slippery road.

Some horses, such as Hackneys, whose main sphere of activity today is the show ring, or the trotters which are used in what is a highly professionalized international sport, have been bred for many generations to excel in this pace, particularly in harness. Whereas the riding horse is happiest and at its most comfortable in a canter, the trotting horse prefers to trot, even under saddle, and heredity and environment have made it reluctant to break into a canter, which is an unaccustomed pace and one, therefore, which does not come naturally to it. Old Shales, from which many famous Hackney strains of the present day derive, held a trotting record of 17 miles an hour, which was a remarkable speed, considering the bad roads which existed at that time. Phenomena, which stood only 14.2 hands high, trotted four miles in less than eleven minutes in 1800. The action at the trot

of the harness horse bred for trotting is vastly different to that of the good quality riding horse.

Horses in their wild state seldom trot, preferring either to walk or to canter. They are inclined to use the trot merely as a transitional pace, unless they are tired. But this does not apply to ponies–Dartmoor ponies, for example–which in their wild state are often to be seen ranging across open spaces at the trot.

Trotting uphill slowly is an excellent exercise for making a horse fit and well muscled. It is, indeed, the pace at which most exercising is done, as far as hunters and even racehorses are concerned, as an alternative to the walk. But although trotting down a line of cavalletti (low poles for jumping) is an excellent schooling exercise, jumping fences out of a trot, which involves a violent transition of pace, is not a comfortable exercise for the novice rider and generally results in his being 'left behind', and causes damage to the horse's mouth. When schooling a young horse, circling at the trot is an essential exercise, as it makes the horse supple and balanced and enables it to progress to faster work. This takes time but a young horse should never be rushed.

Although the canter in the well-schooled horse is the most comfortable pace of all for the rider, novices should not progress to this stage until they have mastered the trot and are both comfortable and in control at this pace. Indeed, a horseman derives just as much interest and enjoyment at the walk, especially with a young horse. It is a relaxed pace, and one at which a surprising amount of valuable schooling can be achieved, in so far as teaching the horse to respond and to carry itself correctly, is concerned. There is a great deal of truth in the saying that, though any fool can ride a horse at a gallop, it takes a horseman to ride it correctly at any other pace.

Below: The trot is a pace in two-time on alternate diagonals. The right diagonal consists of the off-fore and near-hind hooves touching the ground simultaneously; the left diagonal consists of the near-fore and off-hind touching the ground together

Horse movement: canter and gallop

WHEN riding a well-made and well-schooled horse, the canter is the one pace about which it is possible to become positively lyrical. The sheer comfort and delight to be derived from riding such a horse at this pace is an experience never to be forgotten.

In comparison, the canter of an ordinary horse may appear humdrum; it is simply a natural progression from the trot to a faster speed. Yet this is far from being a true canter. Whereas the trot is a pace in two-time, the canter is a pace in three-time. This is the basic difference, but there is more to it than this simple distinction, for the canter is undoubtedly the most intricate and difficult pace to perform well, both for rider and horse.

The gallop, which many people incorrectly believe to be a faster version of the canter, is in fact a movement in four-time. Apart from the racecourse and the hunting field when hounds are running, the gallop is generally reserved for the polo field and for competitive riding such as show jumping, hunter trials and one- and three-day events.

In the canter, one pair of fore- and hind-legs is always in front of the other or 'in the lead', and whichever foreleg strikes the ground first is known as 'the leading leg'. When moving in a circle in a clockwise direction, the horse will lead with the off-foreleg. When cantering to the left it will lead with the near-fore, or inside leg. If it is leading with the wrong leg it may well find itself in difficulty on corners and will risk falling.

If the horse is leading with its off-foreleg, the off-hindleg and the near-foreleg will touch down together. When it leads with the near-fore, the near-hind and the off-fore will touch down together. In the

The canter is a movement in three-time and is the most difficult pace for both horse and rider. The gallop (inset) is in four-time and is very exhilarating

Above, this page and opposite: the canter in which the rider should sit low in the saddle, the upper part of the body moving gently with the motion of the horse

first case it is on the off-lateral and in the second on the near-lateral. It is then said to be cantering 'united', in the true canter. When it changes the lateral, and thus the leading leg, while cantering, this is called a 'flying change'.

If it changes the lead of one leg without changing the lead of the hindleg of the same lateral, so that it is, for example, leading with its near-leg behind and its off-leg in front, it is said to be cantering 'disunited'.

In both the canter and gallop there is a split second when all four feet are off the ground at the same time. In the canter this moment occurs between the third time of one stride and the first of the next. In the gallop it happens between the fourth and the first times.

The canter is the pace which is in most general use by experienced horsemen, whether it be in the hunting field, the show jumping arena or the sphere of horse trials. It is the easiest pace for the horse, provided that it is fit, and the most comfortable for the rider, once he has learned to sit down in the saddle, which many novices find difficult. On some horses it is indeed hard to sit down at all, but on others conformation and movement are such that the rider can sit into the middle of the back, as if part of the horse.

In the dressage arena a great deal of the work is done from the canter: changing legs at every third, second and, finally, at every stride, performing a pirouette and so on. In the show jumping ring every fence is jumped out of a canter, with frequent adjustments made to the length of the horse's stride in order to assist it to make the best possible take-off, particularly with combination fences.

The canter is a far more exciting and exhilarating pace for the horse than either the walk or the trot. However, the canter is not, or should not be, a fast pace, although the 'extended' canter is, of course, performed at a faster speed than the 'collected' canter. In the show ring,

a 'hack' canter is a very elegant movement which is often actually slower than the trot, and it is the epitome of light and sympathetic control. It is, in fact, the true horseman's pace, and it can either reveal glaring faults in its exponents, both human and equine, or provide proof of their expertise.

It is while cantering that a young or over-fit horse, particularly on a wild and windy day, is tempted to indulge in such unseating exploits as bucking, or perhaps shying in mock alarm as a bird flies out of a nearby hedge. So it is essential for the rider to start off with a fair amount of steadying work at the walk and trot.

The same is even truer of work at the gallop, which can often turn into a race, if executed in company. This is a situation which novice riders should be strenuously careful to avoid in case their horses get out of control. Any horse of mettle loves to gallop with its fellows, but to be run away with is not at all a pleasant sensation from the rider's viewpoint. At this stage he might more correctly be described as a passenger, and in such a situation must give way to a feeling of utter helplessness.

Horses who have spent their early years on the racecourse, and particularly those whose mouths have been damaged by heavy-handed stable lads, often find it difficult to forget the excitement of their life in a racing stable. Thoroughbreds are not, in any case, suitable for novice riders. Their temperament is too volatile and their reactions too quick for them to be controlled by an inexperienced rider.

Although a rider should sit down in the saddle at the canter, if he does so at the gallop he will impede his horse's progress and his weight on the loins will cause the horse to tire very rapidly. Perhaps the best seat at the gallop is that employed in the hunting field. Here the rider, in moving his centre of balance forward, allows his seat to rise clear of the saddle and maintains his position by putting his weight on his knees.

Below, this page and opposite: the gallop in which the rider should not touch the saddle, as this tires the horse, but grip with his knees and rest on the stirrups

Schooling a young horse or pony

IT is natural for horses and ponies to jump to a degree, and most have the ability to leap over small obstacles such as ditches and banks that they find in their path. Some, however, possess this ability to a greater degree than others, and can jump higher and wider than their fellows. Thus, though the novice horse needs to learn to take care of itself when jumping—and growing experience will teach it when to be bold and when to be wary—what man has to teach it is how to carry weight, in the form of a rider, over an obstacle, and to develop judgement in the approach and take-off.

The first jumping lessons should be given when one is dismounted, the horse simply being led over a pole which is laid flat on

the ground. The horse should be encouraged to step over it, taking the obstacle in its stride, rather than jumping it. It should not be allowed to become excited. To this end, it is better to leave the jumping until the end of each schooling period when the horse has settled down and is working kindly and quietly. No horse should be taught to jump without adequate basic schooling, or it will not be able to interpret or act upon the instructions it is given. It must be fit and supple so that the hocks are fully engaged; unless they are well under, the horse will not be in a position to use them to propel itself forward and upward simultaneously.

Once the horse allows itself to be lunged quietly over the pole, in either direction, it should be allowed to progress to the next stage, which is working over cavalletti. Cavalletto (the singular form) is a word meaning 'little horse', and was the invention of Captain Umbertrillo, an Italian show jumping rider and instructor in the years between the two wars. It consists of two X-shaped trestles connected by a stout pole of between 9 and 10 feet long. The pole

No horse should be taught to jump without adequate basic schooling which will make it fit and supple. The first stage is to lunge the horse over a pole which is laid flat on the ground

is fixed in the 'V' of the trestle so that it can be set at three heights, usually 10 inches, 15 inches and either 18 or 19 inches. Cavalletti are now used in most, but by no means all, schools of equitation. A series of cavalletti is an invaluable item of equipment; they can be placed at different distances as the horse gains experience, and can be used to accustom the horse to jump a series of fences. One will suffice in the early stages of training; the horse should be lunged over it, or driven over it in long reins, at the end of each schooling session.

It is very important that the horse should learn to jump in good style from the very beginning—that is, to lower its head in the last strides before taking off, and then to describe a parabola over the fence itself: to *bascule*, as the French say. This means that the horse's spine is bent into a convex shape, like a whip. A horse that jumps with its head held high and its back straight or, worse still, concave, has to put far more effort into the jump. Such a horse will not, in most cases, be able to jump so high, though there are freak horses which habitually jump like stags and get away with it. But they are exceptions.

In a large establishment one would expect to find a loose jumping lane, where the horses can learn to look after themselves over a series of fences both before and after they are asked to carry a rider over a fence. The private individual is not so fortunate and must rely on the use of cavalletti and, later, on post-and-rails and brush fences.

In order that the horse should jump freely on the lunge it is necessary for the trainer to carry a long lunge whip. The whip, however, is not (or should not be) used other than to flick behind the horse should it think of stopping or running out. If a greater degree of encouragement proves necessary, a flick that touches the horse under the point of the hock should be sufficient.

It is important that the fences should be as solid as possible. Horses do not learn to respect bean sticks, but if they rap their legs on solid poles they are more careful the next time. Nonetheless, young horses should be schooled in protective bandages.

As in all things connected with the horse's training, it must not be hurried or over-faced (asked to jump a height outside its range) or it will lose confidence. A horse enjoys jumping as long as it does not get frightened or hurt. It should be praised when it has done well. If it suddenly starts to refuse as the fences get bigger, this suggests that the training has been too hurried, and it should be taken back to smaller fences.

When the horse is jumping a height of three feet with ease and enjoyment, it may be taken back to the beginning and accustomed to jumping with a rider on its back. It is essential to use a neck strap to avoid interfering with the mouth at this vital stage in a horse's education. A young horse will often approach a fence incorrectly and make an awkward jump in order to keep out of trouble. If the rider is 'left behind' and gives it a jab in the mouth each time this happens, the horse will soon associate jumping with discomfort, if not actual pain, on the sensitive bars of its mouth where the bit rests. Nothing will put it off jumping more quickly and make it start refusing. Take it back to the pole on the ground, first at the walk, then at the trot, and then on to the cavalletti at all three heights progressively. Strong leg aids are important if the horse shows any sign of trying to stop or run out. After jumping, show that you are pleased. When it takes the fence in its stride from the trot, without losing cadence, a second cavalletto may be introduced, and the distance between them varied. The horse will learn to use its hocks and to pick its feet up. Now try using a third cavalletto, then a fourth, placing the cavalletti at a distance of between 4 and 6 feet apart when working at trot. The exact distance depends, of course, on the individual horse's length of stride. This exercise makes the horse balanced and supple.

Below: a horse must clear 3 feet while being lunged before being mounted

In a week or so the horse will be ready for bigger fences and may graduate to a post-and-rails, some 18 inches high. A pole should also be placed on the ground, slightly in front of the higher pole, to act as a ground-line and help the horse to take off at the right time. During this entire period of training it is very useful to have a dismounted assistant who can move poles about, replace them when they are knocked down, build cavalletti and so on.

Cavalletti should still be used until training is quite advanced, for this type of work strengthens and encourages the engagement of the hind legs and helps the horse to round its back. If the horse tends to rush fences, put a low cavalletto some 24 feet in front of the take-off side. Up to the height of 2 feet 6 inches all work should be done at the trot until, with practice, it becomes as nearly perfect as possible.

It is impossible to over-emphasize the importance of keeping all jumping lessons short and progressive. As soon as the horse has done correctly what is asked of it, leave well alone until the following day. There is a great temptation to advance too rapidly when things are going well, but it should be resisted at all costs. Horses can become soured very easily, and a young horse of four years old can tire quite quickly, with the attendant risk of strain upon its legs, which are still immature. Half the troubles with horses are caused by trainers being too ambitious and in too great a hurry. It is far better to advance too slowly than to rush the horse's training and to skimp the essential groundwork which is the foundation of every well trained horse.

When the horse is happy and confident over 2 feet 6 inches, the time has come to teach it to jump out of a canter. It is a good plan to revert to the lunge for the first few lessons. Then it may be remounted and trotted up to within ten strides of the fence before breaking into a canter without increasing the pace. Do not forget to use the neck-strap at take-off, giving the horse complete freedom of head and neck in order to preserve its balance.

The fences should now be varied with the introduction of oil drums, perhaps a wall and a low hurdle with a pole on top of it. It is also time to introduce spread fences. The easiest to negotiate is the triple bar, which is built on the staircase principle, with the near pole on the ground, the second one at 2 feet 6 inches, and the far one at 3 feet, with an overall spread of 3 feet 6 inches. A horse invariably finds this an easy obstacle. It is the parallel bar which is more difficult but actually teaches a horse to bend its back as no other type of fence can do.

It is as well to start off with a false parallel—that is, with the near pole some 6 inches lower than the far one, so that the horse can see each of them clearly in the approach. A low cavalletto will provide a groundline and encourage the horse to stand back. It should then progress to the true parallel.

When all stages have been mastered the horse will be able to jump a double bar

Preparation for jumping the water type of spread fence should bring cavalletti into play once again, set 2 feet apart so that the horse takes them in its stride, and at their lowest height. The distance between them can be increased to 4 feet, and then to 6 feet, with a 12 inch one set in the middle to encourage it to jump both wide and a little higher. The horse should come into the fence at a strong collected canter and should accelerate in the last three strides. The timing of take-off is indeed the most crucial part of the negotiation of any fence, and it is important never to get too close. The best show jumping riders know this point to an inch, and will place their horses and ask them to take off there. But the novice rider and young horse have to learn to feel this for themselves. The rider should follow a policy of non-interference and leave the point of take-off to the horse, sitting well forward, maintaining plenty of impulsion with the legs and leaving the head free in the last strides.

Training your horse to jump

WHEN the basic essentials of jumping have been mastered, and the young horse or pony jumps small fences freely and easily and appears to enjoy itself in the process–and it is very important that it should demonstrably enjoy every part of this work–its owner may well decide that they should enter for competitive events in which the negotiation of obstacles forms an integral part.

This does not necessarily mean show jumping. Many horses that jump well over small or medium sized fences are still a long way removed from any pretensions to being show jumpers, a name which implies a specialized ability to jump sizeable obstacles. The true show jumper is, indeed, something of a freak. A very well-known rider and trainer of show jumpers, through whose hands many thousands of horses have passed during the course of a long life, has said that if he found one show jumper in every two thousand horses who passed through his yard, it would be the maximum he could hope for.

There are other activities, less high-powered, in which the owner of a reasonable performer can amuse himself and at the same time improve the ability and the standard of training of his mount. First and foremost there is the hunting field. To the initiated, hunting is probably the finest of all sports involving the horse. It provides its followers with fresh air, exercise, companionship and excitement, not the excitement of hunting down a living creature, but of involvement in a risk sport and the thrill of riding across country on a good horse. But the hunting field is not the place to teach a horse to jump. This is a job that must be done at home. To school a horse over fences while out hunting is to court disaster, not to mention the anger of the Master of Foxhounds when claims for broken fences come in.

The horse who has not learned to look after itself when jumping can never be an enjoyable, nor even a safe conveyance in the hunting field. So, in addition to schooling over cavalletti and different fences at home, each with its own inherent problem, no opportunity should be lost to pop over small ditches and banks during the course of exercise. In some parts of the country this is easier said than done. But none of the fences encountered in the hunting field will bear any resemblance to those found in the covered school or in a jumping field. Natural fences almost invariably have some problem of approach or siting. They may have a drop, or an uphill or downhill approach, the going may be trappy or there may be overhanging branches. Most horses like to jump, and a horse that is inclined to be impetuous, and to rush its fences, will learn to go carefully if it is accustomed to popping over any suitable obstacles that it meets in the course of its daily round.

For the more ambitious, there are hunter trials or even one-day events. The former require less expertise, in that neither a dressage test nor a show jumping course are included. A hunter trial course consists of some dozen or more natural cross-country fences, spread out over a mile or so of farmland and well within the compass of any reasonable hunter. Rounds are timed, with victory going to the fastest clear round, but it is possible to canter round at a fair hunting pace, and still to win a rosette.

One-day events are another matter. The fences are not intended to be natural, and if many of them were met during the course of a normal day's hunting, then many of the youngsters and elderly people who enjoy their hunting might well decide to take up a different sport forthwith. The one-day event is the nursery for the three-day event, such as those held at Badminton and Burghley. The three-day event is designed to test the *complete* horse and rider–the combination, in fact, which can perform an adequate dressage test, jump a two-mile steeplechase course, and (as part of a 17 to 20 mile speed and endurance test) negotiate some 35 cross-country fences safely before jumping a further course of show ring fences on the final day. It therefore lies well beyond the scope of this article, even at Pony Club level.

The first essential in any riding horse is free forward movement, and this is particularly so in the negotiation of fences. Of paramount importance, too, is obedience to hand and leg, in order to enable the rider to shorten or to lengthen his horse's stride as occasion demands. Both these requirements are based upon adequate schooling on the flat, without which neither a relaxed performance, nor a co-operative frame of mind, can be induced in the horse. If the horse is strung up and excited, or if it is constantly trying to impose its will on the rider (rather than vice versa) the necessary accuracy and precision will not be attained. A generous temperament is half the battle and makes the trainer's task far easier, but even a difficult horse eventually learns to accept discipline with a good grace if it is tactfully but firmly administered.

Rushing is a common fault among excitable horses. To correct this, they must be given quiet, disciplined schooling. The horse should not be schooled over a line of fences but circled close to a single jump.

Finding a horse that will turn into a good jumper may be a life's work, as such horses are comparatively rare.

When it is sufficiently calm, the fence can be included in the circle. It is important that the rider does not 'telegraph' his intention to take the fence on that particular circuit to the horse, so that it will remain absolutely calm. The fence should only be jumped when the horse is balanced and the approach is absolutely right. Even when the horse is going calmly the fence should not be jumped every time, and the ratio of jumps to circles should probably never exceed one to three or four. When the exercise is first begun it may be necessary to circle the horse in front of the jump as many as twelve times before it can be jumped once.

In many cases, this fault has been caused by a nervous and insecure rider, who takes a tighter hold of the reins, or may even pull, when approaching the fence. The rider must learn to keep his hands steady and not increase the pressure on the reins. The cure is often to jump the horse on a loose rein; it will remain calm and not try to fight its rider.

It is a great advantage for a young horse to have an equine schoolmaster to teach by example. Horses are gregarious animals that enjoy working in company with others, and their herd instinct encourages them to follow a leader. Many horses that are reluctant to jump in cold blood are perfectly happy to do so in the hunting field, when given a lead.

Most horses are natural jumpers, up to a certain height, and so the only unnatural thing to which it must learn to adjust is of jumping with a weight on its back. Before the great Italian instructor, Federico Caprilli, initiated the forward seat which revolutionized the technique of riding over fences, riders sat back on their horses' loins, well behind the natural centre of gravity, and this weight impeded their mounts. Now that riders all over the world are taught to sit forward over their fences, the rider's weight is distributed over the strongest part of the horse's body and does not interfere with his natural balance or equilibrium unless things go very wrong in the approach or the take-off.

A horse's natural instinct for self-preservation soon teaches it to look after itself and to avoid falling wherever possible. If it makes a bad mistake and nearly comes down, it learns a lesson which it will not forget and which seldom needs to be repeated. For this reason, many people believe in lungeing over fences in the preliminary stages, and having recourse to jumping lanes, in order that the horse may learn to cope with minor problems without a weight on its back. Others argue that as the rider's

Three-day eventing tests the technique and courage of both horse and rider in all aspects of riding.

weight will have to play its part sooner or later, the horse should be ridden over fences from the beginning.

There are several common causes of bad jumping and refusals. One is lack of proper training, the horse having been asked to jump fences that are too large and difficult for the stage in its training it has reached. If a horse has had one or more bad falls, it may lose its nerve and begin refusing to jump. A horse that is weak and in poor condition should never be asked to jump, as jumping requires a great deal of energy and the horse may injure itself and its rider because it cannot make the required effort to clear the fence. It is also important to make sure that the horse is not suffering from any leg or foot complaints, such as splints or pulled tendons. If it is, then seek the advice of a veterinary surgeon and do not jump the horse again until he is completely satisfied with the horse's recovery. Also check that the saddle and bridle fit correctly and are not causing the animal discomfort. This should, of course, always be checked before the horse is ridden. A horse may start refusing to jump because it can remember having pain inflicted upon it when its rider was 'left behind' over a jump and it received a severe jab in its mouth. Interference by the rider during the approach to the fence, bad presentation of the horse to the fence, and lack of determination on the part of the rider can all play their part in making a horse jump badly, or even refusing to jump at all.

Perhaps the whole question may be said to hinge upon the expertise of the rider. If he rides well enough to be sure of going with his horse in whatever circumstances, and is able to make rapid adjustments to his seat and hands and general position in an emergency, mounted schooling over fences is to be recommended from the start. If, when the horse makes a mistake, he is liable to get 'left behind' and give his horse an ugly and painful jab in the mouth, he could well destroy a youngster's confidence so that it associates jumping with frustration and discomfort. Until a rider has achieved an independent seat he should confine himself to riding 'made' animals, rather than embarking upon the specialized task of training a young one.

A promising young horse should be trained by a professional if it is to attain the standard needed to reach the top

Becoming an experienced jumper

A horse which has received a reasonable amount of basic training (including suppling and balancing work), which is sufficiently responsive to hand and leg to jump small fences with freedom and enjoyment, and which is reasonably calm and controllable when being ridden over fences, is quite capable of jumping small courses at riding club level. It may then, allowing for time and experience, be able to compete in Foxhunter competitions, designed to encourage hunting people to jump their horses in the show ring and to further the education of novice horses.

The Pony Club and riding clubs exist to provide instruction for children and for novice riders, many of whom are only able to ride in the school holidays or at weekends. They contribute a great deal to the vastly improved standard of riding which now prevails throughout the country at all levels. There is no doubt that the novice horse owner's lot, and that of his

mount, has improved very much since riding clubs started to provide for the adult novice (at a very small annual subscription) the sort of expert instruction and opportunity for competitive riding which the Pony Club has made available to children for the last 50 years. Riding clubs organize instructive lectures, film shows and visits, as well as shows, hunter trials and one-day events, all of which have classes suited to both novice riders and novice horses. Riding club events can provide an excellent introduction to competition work – the courses are unlikely to be large and will not over-face a young horse. Many clubs hold instructional rallies where expert advice can be obtained if you are experiencing any difficulty with training.

One of the major differences between show jumping and every other form of jumping lies in the proximity of the fences and the related distances between them. These distances are worked out for the stride of the average horse, which means that the horse with a long stride or the one with a short stride will have to adjust accordingly if it is to approach a fence with a reasonable certainty of getting over it. Bearing this in mind, the value of basic training really becomes apparent as it does nowhere else but in the dressage arena.

The West Germans are the most successful show jumping nation in the world, partly because show jumping ranks as a national sport, second in popularity only to football. They are successful not only because their horses are strong and powerful and bred to jump fences, but also because the Germans are great believers in their own form of dressage, which insists on complete domination of the horse, which is expected to show instant obedience at all times. Their horses are schooled on the flat to a very high standard, and they insist particularly on a high degree of impulsion and a low head carriage with great suppleness of the neck and back muscles. Balance and suppleness are the primary requisites of the show jumper, together with great impulsion, so that the horse resembles a compressed spring before it takes off.

Caprilli, who innovated the forward jumping seat, believed in leaving all problems of approach for the horse itself to deal with. This principle of non-interference involved riding it over small fences on a loose rein. None of the world's top riders would agree with this today. It is easy enough over small fences, but the modern show jumping course contains too many problems for the horse alone to resolve. Fences are a great deal bigger and wider than they were when the sport was in its infancy. At the time when Caprilli wrote, little was known about distances or distance problems.

As the sport has become more sophisticated its demands have become greater. Today it is more than ever a combined effort, as both mount and man strive to pit their skill and experience into attacking the course that has been built to defeat them. This spirit of co-operation is essential in all forms of riding, but even more so in show jumping. The world's best partnerships are those which steer a middle course between the utter domination of the German school and the opposing non-interference theory of Caprilli. The horses are obedient, but in the case of the rider proving fallible – and even the best make mistakes at times, as they are only too ready to admit – the horse still retains enough initiative to help keep them both out of trouble. In an emergency a rider will often slip the reins with a gesture which says in effect: 'Come on, help yourself. I have done all I can – now it is up to you!' The horse that is accustomed to relying implicitly upon its rider will merely be confused, but the one whose natural instincts have not been completely subjugated will do its utmost to save the situation of its own accord.

Unrelated fences are those which are set at 80 feet or more away from one another, sometimes with a change of direction between them. This type of fence can be treated separately from the standpoint of stride arrangement and control. Where fences are related, the safe negotiation of the second and third fences depends very largely upon a free getaway after landing over the first. Related fences may be set from between 80 feet to 39 feet 4 inches apart.

Closely related fences, namely those spaced within 39 feet 4 inches from each other, constitute double or treble combinations that are the most difficult of all. Individually, a true parallel is the most demanding fence to jump. A combination must be attacked strongly, with maximum impulsion, so that the horse can emerge safely at the other end. Experienced riders always carefully pace out the distances between the various components of a combination on foot during their preliminary inspection of the course. They know that different distances, long or short, require refinements of stride control which only experience and constant practice can teach. For both horse and rider, doubles and trebles are the cause of considerable apprehension, and rightly so. It is all too easy to make a faulty or indecisive approach, jump into a combination and be left inside without a stride to get out. Here the sensible horse will refuse or run out, and have to go back again to the beginning; for to attempt to jump a fence, especially a spread without a

Hard work is essential to attain the standard of such riders as Caroline Bradley on True Love (previous page) and Richard Mead on Wayfarer II (below)

stride and without impulsion, can only end in a fall. And falls shake the confidence of horse and rider alike, as well as making the horse regress and enforcing a return to previous schooling.

In a speed competition, or a timed jump-off, it is not so much the speed at which the horse covers the course that wins events, as the track which the horse follows and its ability to twist and turn in the smallest possible area. Basic schooling is important for this, with plenty of circling and turns to make the horse supple and obedient. A flat-out gallop has no place in the show jumping arena, except perhaps from the last fence to the finish. Excessive speed destroys stride control and precision, causes a horse to flatten its back over fences, can lead to very rough checking which is both ugly and painful for the horse, and spoils many good young horses. A jumping competition should be a test of jumping as such, and must not be allowed to degenerate into a steeplechase. A clever and experienced horse can jump cleanly at speed, but novice horses are capable of only moderate acceleration and should never be pushed beyond their natural rhythm or temperament, otherwise their confidence will suffer.

Lorna Sutherland on Popadom. All the skill of both rider and mount is put to the test in this exacting sport where accuracy and stamina are all important

Experience is acquired the hard way in show jumping, but the best riders do a minimum of actual jumping between competitions, concentrating rather on the essential schooling on the flat. It is quite possible to sicken the keenest horse by endless repetition. If it jumps a schooling fence two or three times in good style, that is enough. On one occasion a rider was seen jumping a practice fence at a show some thirty or forty times. When his turn came to enter the ring, he hit the first fence–the smallest on the course–which indicated that his horse had become bored with the whole operation.

Preparation before the show is very important, particularly for an inexperienced horse. Do not rush its training, and only enter it in a competition when it is absolutely ready. Choose the competition carefully; do not be tempted to put a horse into a class which is too advanced for it, no matter how well it may jump at home. It is often a good idea to take the horse along to a nearby show, not to compete but merely to accustom it to all the noise and excitement.

The build-up to the show should start about three days before. This is not the time to reschool the horse, but merely to brush up the weakest areas of its particular stage of preparation. It should not only be fit enough to meet the demands that will be made on it during the competition, but also be slightly more alert and fresh than normal. This does not mean that the horse should be given large amounts of heating food before the event; it would then be too excitable to be manageable. It should be worked normally until three days before the show. On the third day, have an intensive schooling session, concentrating on the horse's weak points. On the second day, the horse should be given a similar but shorter training session. It is most important not to over-jump the horse in these two days. Concentrate on keeping a young horse balanced and controlled over small jumps. An older, more experienced horse can be taken over a couple of fences larger than those he is likely to meet in the competition, but do not be tempted to do too much. The day before the show should be devoted to calming and relaxing work. It is often a good idea to go for a quiet hack in the countryside, just allowing the horse to stretch its legs. Do not let it become over-excited or it will be jaded on the day of the show. Arrangements for travelling to the show should be made well in advance, so that both you and your horse arrive calmly and comfortably. If hacking to the showground, leave in plenty of time so the horse can be rested before its class begins, travelling quietly so the horse remains quiet.

It was very instructive to watch the best riders in the world working their horses during the mornings at the Olympic Games in Munich. They would ride for an hour or more in the sand exercising arenas which abounded at Riem (the equestrian complex outside the city) but they seldom jumped more than six times. Two of the Germans rode their horses in draw reins, and the other two relied on their own good hands to achieve what they wished. Very few riders, of course, ever attain this standard. Show jumping has about one per cent of really outstanding riders and the other 99 per cent keep the sport going. Show jumping today is a full-time job, and a hard one, but hundreds of enthusiasts are content to remain on the fringe of the sport and derive enormous enjoyment from jumping a clear round at their local show. If they can do so on a horse which they have trained themselves, their sense of achievement is increased.

To win a show jumping competition, at whatever level, demands a considerable degree of ability, a reasonable standard of schooling and a large amount of luck. But winning is not everything–the main thing is to put up the best performance of which horse and rider are capable. As a very great instructor used to tell his cavalry pupils: 'Let your performance be memorable for its beauty, win or lose'. The horse would second this sentiment, for ugly riding is bad riding and the horse is the one which suffers.

P

Chapter III
Advanced Riding

What makes a good show jumper?

THERE are so many intangible elements concerned in the make-up of the jumper that no specific definition is really possible. A good show jumper is not, in the first place, recognizable by type, conformation or general proportions, nor by the way he moves and covers the ground; some are long-striding while others are the very opposite, and it does not seem to make much difference to their performance.

Neither is it possible to breed a jumper. It has been tried, of course, but never with any consistent success.

In theory the best physical specimen, perhaps a champion show horse, should have a greater capacity for jumping big fences, both as regards height and spread, than those who are less well-made. In practice this is not always the case. There was, for instance, the Dublin hunter champion sold to the Italians for a large sum as a potential show jumper. Alas, he never left the ground and is reputed to have ended up in the shafts of a water-cart on the Roman streets.

Conversely, there have been jumpers who, in repose at any rate, looked lost without a cart and were yet among the most successful when it came to tackling a course of big fences. The classic example was the horse on which Harvey Smith first gained recognition. This was Farmer's Boy, which exhibited most of the conformational defects and was desperately common to boot. But he had an extraordinary 'pop' in him that took no account of his built-in physical failings.

Those, however, are the extreme examples and it is generally accepted that a top jumper should be physically well-built and display no glaring faults in make and shape. Furthermore, because of the constant travelling which is an inevitable part of modern show jumping, the horse needs a robust constitution if he is to stand up to a full season of competitions.

Size, within reason, seems to be unimportant, and beauty is certainly of no

A good team: horse and rider are calm and confident

Kathie Kussner on Untouchable. It is the character and talent of the rider, as much as the natural aptitude of the horse that makes a good show jumper

account at all. While strength and stamina are obvious essentials, these qualities are by no means directly related to size. On the one hand, for instance, there are the big, powerful German horses, usually of Hanoverian breeding, while on the other it is unnecessary to look further than Marion Mould's diminutive pony, Stroller, who does not measure 15 hh and is yet capable of jumping three rounds of an arduous international course without making a mistake.

It must be concluded, therefore, that if there is one physical factor common to jumpers, regardless of size and shape, it is the possession of an exceptional and natural gymnastic ability. In fact, the show jumper is an athlete comparable to the human counterpart and having the same rare talent.

Nonetheless, physical attributes, however highly developed, are no guarantee of success unless accompanied by a mental toughness of a corresponding standard.

There are many horses, never seen in a jumping arena, who would be physically able to complete a course but are temperamentally unsuited for the sport. Some lack the essential courage, others may be bold enough but are too impetuous to meet the requirements of precision and accuracy demanded by top-class jumping.

The ideal show jumper has an abundance of courage combined with a calm, equable temperament. Without courage of a high order, consistency of performance over courses of international standard will prove unattainable. Similarly, the highly-strung horse, unable to relax, is also unlikely to reach the very top. The continued stress of travel and the tension of big competitions will sooner or later impose too great a strain on his nervous equilibrium and a horse of this kind invariably becomes unmanageable.

There remain two further factors to be considered in the analysis of the successful show jumper.

First, there is the part played by training, the value of which cannot be overestimated. In preparing a horse for any activity, sound, basic training on the flat is a prime requirement for success. Only when this training has been completed is it possible to go on to the more specialized and specific schooling.

The objects of training are to condition the horse both physically and mentally. The former is achieved by exercises designed to develop and supple the muscles in the correct form, to improve natural balance and gymnastic ability and to encourage an effortless fluency in the paces. Mental development is the result of the physical work, producing, if the training is correctly carried out, a calmness of mind and accustoming the horse to the acceptance of discipline and the habit of obedience. With this foundation firmly laid, it is then possible to progress to the more specialized training involved in teaching the horse to jump with maximum efficiency while expending the minimum physical effort necessary to negotiate fences cleanly.

To what point the schooling is carried out varies from one rider to another, as do the methods employed, but all successful riders admit the necessity of good basic training on the flat as part of a jumper's preparation.

The period of time required to produce a top-grade show jumper is dependent upon the individual. Usually, if a horse is backed at three years old and his schooling begun at four, it would be reasonable to expect the horse, if he has sufficient talent, to be competing at five or six years over elementary courses such as are set in the British Foxhunter events. From introductory competitions the horses progress through a system of grading based upon the amount of prize-money won and the amount of success achieved. The standard of the competitions is also taken into consideration.

Few international horses acquire sufficient experience before they are ten years old. Secondly, the influence of the rider has to be considered. Although the style of riding employed varies from nation to nation it stems essentially from one common source—the system of forward riding propounded by the Italian cavalry officer, Captain Federico Caprilli, who lived from 1868 to 1907.

The seat advocated by Caprilli—in which the rider positions his body weight over the moving centre of balance of the horse (that is, he sits forward using a shortened stirrup leather) allowing the horse complete freedom to stretch out head and neck and to arch (*bascule*) over a fence—persists throughout the world today. Caprilli's system, however, involved much more than the rider's seat. It was based, primarily, on the principle of non-interference by the rider with the balance and attitude of the horse. Few nations, if any, now practise the Caprilli system in its entirety. Riders prefer to follow a middle course of part-intervention, a course which, indeed, is made necessary having regard to the complexity and severity of present-day international jumping competitions.

Understandably, the Italian brothers, Raimondo and Piero d'Inzeo, two riders who have been at the top of the show-jumping tree for the best part of a quarter of a century, are possibly the nearest in style and technique to the classical Caprilli system, but on the whole it is the Americans who exemplify more consistently and uniformly the Caprilli style. The American teams, trained by Bert de Nemethy, ride, virtually without exception, to a noticeable pattern. Such riders as Bill Steinkraus, the former American captain and Olympic gold medallist, Frank and Mary Chapot, Neil Shapiro and Kathie Kussner, all ride with a fluency and perfection of style characteristic of the Italian system.

British riders, in general, also follow the principle of part—or half—intervention but are far more individual in the style and seat employed and many of them, including Harvey Smith, are entirely self-taught. Possibly the supreme British stylist and certainly the most experienced of British international riders is Peter Robeson, one of the world's most elegant horsemen.

At the opposite end of the scale are the German riders, men like Paul Schockemohle and the new World Champion, Hartwig Steenken, who are far more demanding of their horses and may be said to practise full intervention, their horses' performance being almost entirely dictated by the rider. The Germans are rarely elegant horsemen but that they are strong and supremely effective is beyond doubt.

Nonetheless, whatever the method or style employed, the final and possibly the supreme factor completing the picture of the show jumper is the influence of the individual rider.

It was once said that even if Harvey Smith was mounted on a donkey he would still be worth a place in a British team—the same would be true of the former World Champion, David Broome. Both these riders, as well as some others, are able to get results from a variety of horses, some of which in less skilful hands would never be classed as better than average.

This has been amply demonstrated by riders of differing styles who have been very much to the fore in recent years—Rodney Jenkins of the USA on Number One Spy; Eddie Machen of Ireland on Oatfield Hills; John Cottle of New Zealand on Warlock VII; Caroline Bradley of Britain on True Lass and Middle Road and Anne Moore of Britain on Psalm.

Harvey Smith, for instance, is adept at taking a horse that has previously been no more than an ordinary performer and bringing it to international level within an extraordinary short space of time. David Broome is little short of a genius in persuading all kinds of horses to go kindly for him. One of his early horses was Wildfire, a 'throw-out' that had gone sour, but which in David's hands became a reliable and almost brilliant international horse.

Peter Robeson expends endless patience and time to produce a show jumper. His Olympic horse, Grebe, is an example of the quiet careful preparation that is characteristic of this rider.

Less successful riders—lacking, perhaps, the mental make-up that is as necessary for the rider as for the horse—may have the best of horses but will be unable to realize their potential. They may, if they are sufficiently wealthy, buy established high class jumpers—only to find that a horse that won at the Royal International under a Broome, a Smith or a Robeson is not in the same class when ridden by themselves.

So it is undoubtedly the character and talent of the rider, just as much as any natural aptitude of the horse, that makes a good show jumper. It is not, of course, an aptitude that can be developed quickly in a horse. As Bill Steinkraus, the former American Olympic rider and international authority on riding, has written: 'For the sport of riding (and even more, the art) yields its secrets slowly; and just as baseball pitchers are said to 'only really learn to pitch' when they've lost their fast ball, many riders only really think about their sport when they have to utilize time with some economy and make the most of limited opportunities.'

White Lightning, here ridden by Mary Chapot (USA), has abundant courage plus a calm temperament—essential qualities in a jumper

Horse Trials

HORSE trials comprise the ultimate test of the well-trained horse and rider. In Britain they are known as the Three-day Event or combined training, and on the Continent as the *concours complet*, (the complete test) or the Militaire, as these tests originated as trials for cavalry officers and their chargers. At first they were simply endurance tests for both mount and man over long distances. They were included in the Olympic Games for the first time at Stockholm in 1912, and in 1920 they were opened to civilian riders in addition to the military riders. It was not until 1926 that they assumed the form they now take. All three-day events conform to the rules of the Fédération Equestre Internationale (FEI) which is the governing body which controls all affairs concerning international equestrian sports.

The three-day event is divided into three parts. Initiated by the dressage test, which riders perform from memory, it continues on the crucial second day with the speed and endurance test – the most important and decisive part of the event – and concludes with show jumping.

The speed and endurance test is in itself composed of four distinct divisions. Phase A consists of the first section of roads and tracks along a marked course. Phase B consists of a steeplechase course. Phase C is the second, and longer, section of roads and tracks. It is followed by a 10-minute break for a compulsory veterinary inspection before horse and rider are allowed to set off on the most testing part of all, Phase D, the cross-country course.

At the 1972 Olympic Games in Munich, which may be accepted as the definitive test, Phase A was run over a course of 3,600 metres at a speed of 240 metres per minute. The time allowed was 15 minutes and the time limit 18 minutes. The time allowed is the time which would be taken if the course were ridden at the speed laid down in the conditions. Were it to be covered in a faster time, no bonus points would be awarded, though penalty points could accrue for exceeding the time allowed, on the scale of one point for each commenced second in excess of the time

allowed, until the time limit was reached (the limit being one-fifth longer than the time allowed). Competitors exceeding the time limit were eliminated.

Phase B, the steeplechase, also run over 3,600 metres at a speed of 600 metres a minute, had a time allowed of 6 minutes and a time limit of 12 minutes. Here bonus points were awarded for good times, to a maximum of 37·6. The best time was laid down at 5 minutes 13 seconds. Again, penalty points were awarded for exceeding the time allowed,

Right: HRH the Princess Anne on Goodwill during the Badminton Horse Trials in April 1973. Far left, below: Richard Meade and Laurieston at Badminton in 1972

on the ratio of 0·8 for each commenced second up to the time limit, which was twice the time allowed. Bonus points for finishing under the time allowance were 0·8 for each commenced second up to a speed of 690 metres in the minute, which produced the best time of 5 minutes 13 seconds.

Both here and in the cross-country, penalties were also incurred for faulting at obstacles, on the same scale in each phase. A first refusal, run-out or circle cost 20 penalty points. A second at the same obstacle cost 40 (totalling 60) and a third entailed elimination. Falls were also penalized, with 60 for the first fall of horse or rider, and elimination for a second fall in Phase B or a third fall in Phase D. Faults at obstacles, however, were only counted if they occurred within the penalty zone which was marked out at each obstacle. This began 10 metres in front of the fence, stretching over its entire width to a distance of 10 metres out from each side, and extended 20 metres beyond it.

Horse Trials, otherwise known in Britain as the Three-Day Event, are a tough test for both horse and rider

Phase C, the second part of the roads and tracks, was considerably longer than the first, being run over 15,120 metres with a time allowance of 63 minutes and a limit of 75 minutes 36 seconds. Scoring was the same as for Phase A.

The cross-country course in Munich was 8,100 metres long and included 36 obstacles. The speed was set at 450 metres per minute, the time allowed was 18 minutes and the limit 36 minutes. The best time was 14 minutes 13 seconds, the maximum possible bonus points were 90·8, and 0·4 penalty points were incurred for each second over the time allowed, up to the time limit. Exceeding the time limit entailed elimination. Bonus points of 0·4 were awarded for each second in which the course was completed under the time allowed, up to a speed of 570 metres per minute (120 metres per minute faster than the speed laid down).

On the following morning, another veterinary inspection is compulsory for the horses still remaining in the competition–those who have not retired, withdrawn, or incurred elimination. In the afternoon, the third part of the Event, the show jumping, commences. The course is in no way comparable to that set for a conventional Olympic or international show jumping competition, as its whole purpose is simply to prove that the horse remains sound, supple and obedient after its gruelling trial.

Thus there are only 10 or 12 fences on a course which may vary between 750 and 900 metres. The speed is 400 metres a minute, and the maximum allowable height and spread are respectively 1·20 and 1·80 metres. Penalties are incurrable on the following scale: 10 for the first disobedience (refusal, circle or run-out), 20 for the second and elimination for the third. Each knockdown or water fault costs 10 penalties, a fall of horse or rider costs 30 points, and jumping a fence in the wrong order or failing to correct an

error of course entails elimination. No bonus points are available for completing the course in less than the time allowed, but 0·25 of a penalty point is given for each commenced second of overtime up to the time limit. Exceeding the time limit entails elimination.

This form of test is the basis for every three-day event in the world. It is a tough assignment for any horse and entails peak performance, condition and fitness on the part of both horse and rider. For this reason few horses are entered for more than two three-day events in the year. Only four are held in England – at Badminton, Tidworth (the preserve of the less experienced horses) Burghley, and Bramham Moor. Few British international horses compete in more than one national event each year. The reason is that they will also be called upon to make up the team for the Olympic Games or the World Championship every four years, and for the European Championship (or, in the Western hemisphere, the Pan-American Games) in the two intervening years.

British horses and riders have led the world in horse trials from 1954 until 1960 and again from 1967 until the present time. They have won three sets of Olympic team gold medals (in 1956 at Stockholm, in 1968 in Mexico City and in 1972 at Munich) and a British rider, Richard Meade with Major Derek Allhusen's home-bred Laurieston, holds the individual gold medal. He is the first-ever British winner of an Olympic gold medal in equestrian sport. The United States, which has a long and distinguished record in this sport, is the second-best in the world and was runner-up to Britain both in Mexico and Munich, winning the team silver medals.

British horses and riders are ideally suited to this form of competition, which did not start in England until the Duke of Beaufort started the Three-day Event at Badminton in 1949. The British tradition of fox-hunting has produced riders who excel across country and horses which have been bred to this demanding sport for many generations. They are stronger and tougher, with more speed and stamina than horses of any other country. Their conformation and quality are also superior to those of any other nation except Ireland.

For this reason they are in great demand in every country. Both the West German and the United States teams are reinforced by British horses, and two of the four West German horses which won the Olympic bronze medals in Munich were bred and produced in England. The United States Olympic team fielded one British and one Irish horse, both of them still fit and sound after five years of international competition.

Mr H Kingsley on Aeolia at the Crookham Trials during the cross-country section, the hardest and most important part

In Britain, a valuable nursery for horses and riders of the three-day event is provided by the one-day event. Almost all of these are sponsored by the Midland Bank, and they are held all over the country from March to October, attracting so many entries that they are frequently over-subscribed and horses have to be turned away. Most are held under the auspices of the British Horse Society, under the general control of the Combined Training Group. This is an organization within the BHS which is the controlling authority for combined training affairs in the UK. Its executive committee is made up of members elected by the Group, and nominated by the BHS.

The experience gained over these easier courses is valuable, and young animals are never discouraged by being asked to tackle obstacles of maximum height and difficulty before they are ready. They also receive a thorough grounding in all branches of the sport. Nowadays, children on their ponies can also ride in horse trials as part of the Pony Club inter-branch competition. Eventing is also a sport at which women seem to excel and are able to compete on equal terms. Such riders as Princess Anne, Debbie West, Mary Gordon-Watson and Lucinda Prior-Palmer have become household names through their success at Badmington, Burghley and the Olympic Games.

Riding in point-to-points

POINT-TO-POINTS are races for qualified horses which are certified by a Master of Foxhounds to have been regularly and fairly hunted during the current season. They are so called because they used to be run, quite literally from one point (the start) to another (the finish) over a natural stretch of country, perhaps from a farm to a church tower some three miles away. Many of the courses now used have jumps built into the fencing of the fields over which the races are run, and so have become a permanent feature of the landscape.

Point-to-points were devised both to give sport to the foxhunting fraternity and also to entertain the farmers as a reward for allowing the hunt to cross their land. However, today point-to-points are far more sophisticated affairs, particularly in

the areas south of London and in the Home Counties. Regulation birch fences and a high degree of organization by the Hunt Committee make them resemble nothing so much as a small race meeting complete with bookmakers, a totalisator and refreshments.

Previously, any fit hunter was entered for its local point-to-point, but nowadays the pace is far too fast for anything but a Thoroughbred horse. Many successful pointers (as a point-to-point horse is known) are former steeplechasers which have just failed to make the grade under National Hunt Rules, though the regulations state that they must have been out of training for a year before they are eligible to run in point-to-points. Others, especially in Ireland, are horses which are being schooled over point-to-point fences before going into training for steeplechasing. A few are home-bred horses which are raced by their owners in order that they might graduate to the big hunter 'chases at Liverpool and Cheltenham. Races which are confined to amateurs.

Point-to-points are so called because these races were once just that, a race from one specific place to another over open country

The whole sport of point-to-point racing is strictly amateur, but with safety regulations demanding standardized courses, which are inspected annually. A veterinary surgeon must be in attendance throughout the meeting, and it is normal practice for an ambulance and medical assistance to be present in case of any mishap. There are strict rules regarding the amateur status of jockeys. No one can ride in a point-to-point who has previously held a professional racing licence, or who has ever been paid, directly or indirectly, to ride in a race. No man who has worked in a licensed training stables, hunt or livery stables as a groom or stable lad is permitted to ride until three years have elapsed since his employment there. No woman under the age of 18 is allowed to ride in a point-to-point. No horse under the age of five years can be raced. The Jockey Club can provide more comprehensive details of the requirements for competing in point-to-points.

Until some 25 years ago, local hunts had hunting country where the natural obstacles were predominantly banks, rather than fly fences. They were allowed to run their point-to-points over banks, and as banks have to be jumped slowly, here the genuine hunter was quite capable of winning races, providing it was possessed of sufficient quality. But the high accident rate over such courses resulted in the abolition of the banking meetings which, incidentally, took place chiefly in the West Country. The standard of horses entered in subsequent meetings has become immeasurably higher but it is debatable, however, whether this has resulted in point-to-point meetings remaining anything like as enjoyable as before. The average hunting man or woman stands little chance of winning a race on their hunter, unless it be a race which is confined solely to members of the local hunt, and even here members who own expensive Thoroughbreds will always have the advantage.

The maiden race, full of inexperienced horses, and the Hunt race, in which both horses and riders are generally lacking in experience, provide the most spectacular races of the day. The open race, for the best horses, is the most hard fought, and fastest of the day is the Ladies' race, which is also extremely competitive. A famous steeplechase jockey was heard to say that he would rather take part in the hurly-burly of the Grand National than to take on the competitors of a ladies' race at a Hunt meeting. Many female flat race jockeys have started their careers by riding in point-to-points, and this has proved to be a very good training ground.

Point-to-point horses are usually hunted until Christmas, and must be presented to the Master both at the beginning of the Meet and on departure, which should not be before 2.30 in the afternoon. They are also supposed to take their chance by following hounds, rather than sticking to the safety of the roads and lanes, in order to qualify for their 'regular and fairly hunted' certificate. Once they have earned their certificate, they generally go into training proper, for a horse that has been hunted hard throughout the season, will have nothing left in the spring to gallop fast over three to four miles, even though it will be hunting fit.

If one is to be successful in point-to-point racing, a great deal of preparation must go into getting the horse fit and supple to enable it to withstand the rigours of hunting and racing. Pointers are usually brought up from grass in September and then begins the slow steady process of increasing their food and exercise to bring them into peak condition. The horse should be stabled and exercised six days a week. If it is not possible to exercise the horse every day, then the process of getting it fit will take con-

Originally, point-to-points were devised for members of the local hunt, and also to entertain the farmers who had let the hunt use their land. Nowadays such meetings have become far more sophisticated, and thoroughbred horses take part

siderably longer. The horse that is in full-time work, a bran mash should be given on the evening before a non-work day.

It is essential to formulate a balanced and well-organized programme of diet and exercise which should be strictly adhered to. The amount of food and exercise should be gradually increased each week. In the beginning the horse should be given four pounds of oats, three pounds of chaff (chopped hay) and ten pounds of bulk hay per day. This should be increased so that by the time the horse is in racing condition, it is consuming between ten and fifteen pounds of oats, seven pounds of bran, seven pounds of chaff each day and the amount of hay given has decreased. It is important to maintain a balance between short feed (oats, barley, etc.) and bulk feed (bran and chaff). The measurements given are, of course, only intended to be a rough guide. Some horses will need more corn, some more bulk. The diet should be adjusted to meet the individual requirements of the horse. Judge the success of your regime by the appearance and performance of the horse and make any changes necessary.

Exercise should be started very slowly. If the horse is rushed at this stage it might well break down and be out of action for the rest of the season. The horse should be shod before work commences. Watch carefully for signs of galling under the saddle or girth. This is a common ailment of horses newly brought up from grass. For the first two weeks at least, the horse should be walked for an hour. Short spells of slow trotting can then be introduced. By the fifth or sixth week the horse can be walked for one-and-a-half hours, interspersed with three ten-minute spells of trotting. This should continue until about the eighth week when a short canter can be introduced. In the ninth week, the walking period should be extended to two hours, with thirty minutes trotting and two short canters. By the end of the tenth week the horse should be nearly fit and ready for hunting. A short fast gallop can be introduced at this stage, but it is far more important to concentrate on slow steady work. Trotting slowly and evenly is one of the best ways of toning and firming a horse's muscles, especially the hindquarters. If done up and down hills, the horse will improve even more quickly. Once the hunting season starts, the horse will come into peak condition as his muscles are toned and hardened.

One will notice changes in the horse as its condition improves. Its belly will decrease, while its muscles increase and harden. The profuse lathery sweat of an out-of-condition animal is replaced by a slight dampness on the neck or even nothing at all. To maintain condition while the horse is being hunted or raced, exercise must be continued throughout the week. Do not do more than walk the horse quietly for twenty minutes the day after it has raced. This will take the stiffness out of its joints and reduce any swelling. The next day the normal routine should be resumed.

When a pointer returns from exercise, it should be checked for any signs of lameness, bruises or cuts. The horse should be thoroughly groomed and 'strapped' with a wisp made of straw. This is a form of massage which develops and hardens the muscles, and produces a shine on the coat by squeezing out the oil from the glands in the skin. It stimulates the skin by improving the blood supply. The wisp should be dampened slightly and used vigorously in the direction of the lie of the coat. Special attention should be given to those parts where the muscles are hard and flat, such as the sides of the neck, the quarters and thighs. Avoid applying pressure on bony prominences and the tender loin region.

At the end of the season the horse must be 'roughed-off'. This is the process whereby a fit horse is taken out of work and prepared for a rest at grass. All exercise, grooming and corn feeding should be stopped and the horse given only hay and bran mashes. The blacksmith should be called in to remove the shoes and trim the feet. The horse must be turned out to grass on a mild day. Turn it out while it is still light so that it can inspect its field and find its water supply.

In spite of the popularity of horse trials and combined training events for amateur riders, point-to-points remain as popular as ever. One of the reasons for this continuing appeal is doubtless that no dressage test or show jumping phase is included, and thus a busy farmer's son does not have to dedicate himself to many hours of instruction, in order to ride in his Hunt races. Young men enjoy fast riding–young women too–and and one does not have to be an expert in advanced equitation in order to ride a reasonably adequate horse at speed over regulation fences. To win consistently does, of course, require great application and a certain amount of training, but not all those who engage in point-to-point racing have a win in the Foxhunter's Chase as their ultimate goal. To win a race at their local meeting is triumph enough.

Members and farmers of any hunt are eligible to ride in point-to-points, and many qualify their horses just for the fun of the thing, rather than with any expectation of riding a winner. Simply to complete the course without a fall is the ambition of many, and these are the people who keep the sport alive. It is a sport which provides the hospitable farmers with an enjoyable day out, which builds the character of young riders who are participating in a risk sport with all its inherent challenge and excitement and which ensures the supply of quality horses for every facet of competition riding.

What is dressage?

DRESSAGE is a French word meaning 'training', and a dressage test is, by definition, a test of training in obedience and deportment. It can be as simple as riding a horse in circles round a field to get it balanced and supple, or as complicated as the *Grand Prix de Dressage* in the Olympic Games.

The object of dressage, apart from training a young, unschooled horse to become balanced and obedient, is to lighten the horse's forehand by bringing its hocks under him, where they can be fully engaged in their primary function of providing propulsion and impulsion. The horse in its wild state distributes most of its weight onto its forehand. When it is asked to carry the additional weight of a rider and a saddle, which often totals some 200 lb, it is necessary to centralize the distribution of this extra weight. All training stems from this basic aim. Dressage training encourages the horse to go forward freely and with an even rhythm. This is a prerequisite of a well-schooled horse. It should be alert, balanced and 'on the bit' at all paces. Careful schooling begun when the horse is young, will ensure it has a steady, correct head carriage, its neck flexes correctly, that it moves straight and is completely obedient to the rider's aids. Suppleness, too, is essential if the horse is to perform well the tasks asked of it.

Dressage can either be an end in itself, as among the highest echelons of dressage riders, whose aim is to win dressage competitions, or a means to an end, as in the three-day event or combined training competition. Here, the test is less advanced than in the Grand Prix, and a lower standard is required. The object is to demonstrate that the horse has been schooled to the level which will make it a good and safe ride across country, where it will be able to cope with difficult approaches to fences, jump freely and safely, and prove itself to be a good, all-round performer.

Dressage improves the horse by developing those muscles, particularly in the back and the neck, which are only used by a horse when carrying a rider. A stiff horse is an uncomfortable ride, and only dressage–even if not so termed –produces a horse that is supple and relaxed. The old-time dealers' nagsmen, who spent their lives in 'making' young horses, would have been horrified had they been accused of doing dressage. Yet that is precisely what they did when they encouraged the horse to carry its head in the right place, to bend correctly (or flex) at the poll, to shorten or lengthen its stride, to change the leading leg when cantering, and to perform the elementary movements of training which have always been part of every young horse's education. Even the simple operation of opening and shutting a gate, which is part of every hunter's repertoire, is not achieved without such essential basic training as obedience to the leg, and the ability to stand still without fidgeting and to rein back quietly, in a straight line.

Dressage also imposes discipline upon the horse. A horse which will not obey, which indulges its own wishes and openly defies the will of its rider, has either been insufficiently or incorrectly trained. It is, moreover, a danger to itself, its rider, and anyone else with whom it comes in contact, for it is not under control.

The correct training of a horse, which must be achieved with tact, sympathy and understanding, as well as with firmness, is a slow and gradual process, with no short cuts. Artificial control, achieved by means of gadgets such as tight standing martingales, severe bits, running reins and the like are useless, and indicate impatience or incompetence on the part of the rider. All too soon the horse will learn to evade them in one way or another, and then the last state will be a great deal worse than the first. Hundreds of horses are spoilt because their basic training is either rushed or skimped, and

because they are asked to run before they can walk.

In every dressage test, at whatever level, the movements at each pace – walk, trot and canter – are divided into three different categories: ordinary, collected and extended. The ordinary paces vary, to some extent, with the type of stride and movement of each horse. The horse which has a long stride, is a free mover and seems to 'float' (so lightly does it put its feet down), has a natural advantage over the poorer, often less well-bred, mover and will always receive higher marks. Collection and extension are self-explanatory. The collected movements are obviously performed with a higher degree of control, and therefore with a shorter stride, than the extended movements.

The transitions from one pace to another must be executed smoothly, not jerkily or abruptly, and they are very revealing. The well-trained horse will come to a halt standing four-square, its weight evenly distributed over all four legs. It should be so balanced as to be able to move off immediately at the indication of its rider. If it opens its mouth, this indicates that it is not accepting the bit; if it swishes its tail it is not relaxed.

Such advanced movements as the passage and piaffe, which feature very prominently in the Grand Prix tests, are not included in the three-day event test at all. However, basic faults such as the horse not being straight (its hind legs following in the tracks of its forelegs), or being overbent or inattentive, are penalized just as severely by the judges.

In the three-day event dressage test at the Munich Olympic Games in 1972, work on two tracks, half-circles to right and left and counter-canter were all included in addition to collected and extended walk, trot and canter. Apart from the marks awarded for each movement, the judges assessed the general impression given by each combination in terms of regularity of the paces, impulsion, lightness, obedience of the horse, position and seat of the rider and correct application of the aids. Marks were awarded for each of the 19 movements on the basis of 6 for very good down to 0 (not executed). Each competitor started with 138 penalty points, corresponding to the maximum number of bonus points obtainable. Bonus points awarded during the test were then added to the penalty points, with the remaining penalty points counting towards the final score at the conclusion of the speed, endurance and show jumping phases.

For the Grand Prix dressage the test was far more demanding. It consisted of no fewer than 38 movements, among them pirouettes, four periods of passage and three of piaffe, and changes of leg at every second stride and then at every stride. Of the ten nations entered, the world's chief protagonists at this time – the West Germans (winners of the last three Olympic Games) and the Russians – were the focal points of attention, for their concepts are diametrically opposed. While the Russian idea is based on the French, with lightness of the forehand valued exceedingly highly, the German school is far more dominant, characterized all too often by the fixed head of the horse and the rigid hand of the rider.

Dressage enthusiasts were heartened by the fact that the far more attractive Russian school prevailed on this occasion, the Soviet team taking the gold medals from the West Germans, with the Swedes in third place. But the individual gold medal went to the German lady rider, Liselott Linsenhoff, for her performance on the Swedish-bred horse, Piaff.

Though bad dressage is one of the most boring sights imaginable, and a little dressage goes quite a long way with all but the most dedicated spectators, really top-class performances at Olympic level have considerable fascination for all those who are interested in horses and riding. Dressage enthusiasts are wholly dedicated to their art, are usually highly critical of one another, and have little praise for those whose sport is pursued in the three-day event field or the show jumping arena.

They are, of course, the purists, and that they are also perfectionists goes without saying. Classical riding demands a high standard of self-criticism, and few are ever entirely satisfied with their performances but are always striving to do better. It takes at least five years to train a horse up to the highest level. Thus those who can afford to indulge this taste are either very wealthy or dedicated horsemen, such as those of the Spanish Riding School in Vienna or the French Cadre Noir at Saumur, whose whole working life revolves around training horses in this esoteric art.

These pictures show some of the steps in which the horse is trained. Facing page: extended trot. Above: the horse in a high state of collection. Next page, main picture: the halt, here being done incorrectly as the horse's weight is not evenly distributed. The inserts show, left and right: collected canter; centre: extended canter. The training that is necessary before a horse can carry out these movements correctly improves the horse by toning its muscles and improving its balance

C
FORD
A

High school equitation

HIGH school equitation, which is another term for what is more properly known as classical riding, is practised in the main today at the two last bastions of this fine art – the Spanish Riding School of Vienna, with its Lipizzaners, and the Cadre Noir at Saumur in France. In the sixteenth century, the classical art of riding was at its peak, and riding academies were established at all the royal courts of Europe, but over the years they gradually disappeared.

The Spanish School (formerly the Hofreitschule, or court riding school) is the oldest in the world. It is known as the 'Spanish' school, because of the horses which were sent there from Spain in 1580 to found the Imperial Stud at Lipizza. The Cadre Noir (so called because of the black uniforms worn by the riders) was founded in 1814 when the Royal Cavalry School was created at Saumur at the time of the Restoration. The first instructors, or *Ecuyers*, were civilians from the famous school at Versailles, but during the next 14 years military instructors took over.

In 1840 a civilian with circus connections, Francois Baucher, arrived on the scene with methods based on old classical doctrine, which were later rejected in favour of those promoted by the Comte d'Aure, who wished to extend the school principles into the wider field of cross-country riding. In 1860, when Commandant l'Hotte became *Ecuyer-en-Chef*, a certain compromise was effected and a method evolved which was, by and large, acceptable to both factions – this method remains the basis of today's teaching.

Many writers have expounded the theory of *haute école*, one being the Duke of Newcastle whose 'New Method of Horse Schooling' was published in 1658. François de la Guérinière, known as 'the father of modern horsemanship', published his classical work 'Ecole de Cavelirie' between 1729 and 1733. His book laid the foundations of and described the practice of classical *haute école*. As well as describing the high school airs – *passage*, *piaffe*, *pesade*, *pirouette mezair*, *courbette*, *croupade*, *ballotade* and *caprioles*, he also tried to justify them as being both natural movements and practical ones in warfare. Another very influential writer is Alois Podhajsky, who was for many years Director of the Spanish Riding School in Vienna. His book, 'The Complete Training of the Horse and Rider', describes in detail the development of stallions being trained for their work in the Spanish Riding School. Published in 1967, this book has already come to be considered a classic.

All high school movements are refinements of the natural movements of the horse at liberty, with the difference that they must be produced upon command. Only a horse which has been schooled thoroughly in basic dressage can proceed, through a logical progression of gymnastic exercises, to the high school airs, which are developed through the *passage* and the *piaffe*, and from work on two tracks, to movements 'above the ground' such as the *levade*, the *courbette*, the *croupade* and the *capriole*. These latter, however, are only within the compass of a limited number of horses who, by temperament and natural ability, are particularly suited to these difficult leaps. The Lipizzaner has proved itself to be admirably suited to the performance of these movements.

By its very name, high school work presupposes a very high standard of training. Although it is possible to take short cuts to produce a movement which will impress laymen – such as is frequently, and of necessity, done in the circus – the knowledgeable horseman will not be deceived. Only classical training, which produces the correct balance of the horse and the complete engagement of the hocks from which all movement originates, provides a sure and lasting foundation upon which to build.

High school work is infinitely more difficult to achieve with a temperamental, high-couraged Thoroughbred horse than with the stoical Lipizzaner or other German horses. But the superior quality, the better and more elegant conformation, and the freer movement of the Thoroughbred makes it a better prospect, and a more rewarding one, for this type of work, even though its preparation will demand endless tact and patience. For this reason, most trainers prefer to start on an untouched colt than a horse that has been raced and was possibly badly broken to begin with. The process may take longer, but at least it will be entirely progressive, with no bad habits to be eradicated and less likelihood of the all-important temperament being impaired. On the other hand it has to be recognized that very few Thoroughbred horses are able to accomplish the airs above the ground. For these exercises the conformation and temperament of the Lipizzaner is the ideal.

In terms of the competitive international riding of the present day, high

Right: the levade *is a movement in which the horse rears up from a crouching position with hind legs bent*

school may be said to begin where intermediate dressage leaves off. Some of the movements which are asked for in the Olympic Grand Prix de Dressage are actually high school movements. But no Olympic horse is ever asked to perform anything more complicated than a *passage*, a *piaffe* or a *pirouette*. Work above the ground belongs strictly to the classical riding school. In mediaeval times it was believed that these movements originated in the battlefield, and were used to clear the infantry away from the area. But this belief has recently been called into question, not least because a rearing horse is even more vulnerable to attack by a spearman than is a horse with all four feet on the ground.

These are all artificial movements and can be said to have little use, other than to demonstrate a high degree of training. The *courbette* is a rearing movement with the hind legs straight. The *levade* is a rear with the hind legs bent and the horse in a crouching position. Both the *croupade*, in which the horse stands on his forelegs and kicks out with the hindlegs, and the *capriole*, which incorporates a jump forward and kick out with the hindlegs at the same time, were designated to kick the enemy into retreat. Few amateurs are capable of training a horse to this standard or would, indeed, wish to do so.

In all high school riding the lightness in hand and high degree of precision are obtained by complete collection – the French call it *'rassemble'*, which means literally 'gathered'. A horse which bends its head at the poll, drops its nose and flexes its jaw is collected, and extreme collection to the lightest of aids, so that the horse is perfectly balanced between the rider's hand and leg, is necessary for the cadenced paces required in the advanced school movements.

The *passage* is a slow, very collected and very elevated trot, wherein the horse moves rhythmically from one diagonal to the other. Each diagonal pair of legs is raised and put to the ground alternately, gaining little ground and with an even cadence and prolonged suspension between strides. It should be ridden very slowly, for the shorter the stride, the higher will be the knee and hock movement and the better and longer the period of suspension. It should indeed trot as if on air. Cadence and momentary suspension come first, elevation later. The *piaffe* is, in effect, a *passage* that is done on the spot, without any forward movement that results in gaining ground. It follows that it can be obtained by reducing very gradually the pace of the *passage* until the horse can perform a cadenced trot on the spot. Loss in height inevitably accompanies the loss in pace, but the cadence must remain. The alternative diagonals are raised with even, supple, cadenced and graceful movement, the moment of suspension being prolonged. The height of the toe of the raised foreleg should be level with the middle of the cannon bone of the other foreleg. The toe of the raised hindleg should be slightly lower, reaching just above the fetlock joint of the other hind leg. The *piaffe*, well done, constitutes the maximum possible combination of impulsion and collection. The movement should be supple and harmonious without any swinging of either the forehand or the quarters from side to side.

Even in the Olympic Grand Prix de Dressage one frequently sees a hurried *piaffe*, with neither cadence nor elevation, the result of incomplete or incorrect training. Both *passage* and *piaffe* must be executed slowly and with precision.

The horses used in the Spanish Riding School of Vienna are Lippizaners; their stoicism is ideal for high school work

There is no doubt that high school riding is a very esoteric art, and though in less hurried days courtiers and noblemen, particularly on the Continent, were able to indulge in it, most people today are precluded from achieving any great heights by the sheer necessity of making a living. For it is a time-consuming and dedicated calling, and refinements such as the flying change of leg, which demands absolute straightness on the part of the horse, and the movements already described, take years of patient schooling to achieve.

In more recent years, apart from the two major classical schools at Vienna and Saumur, some of the best high school riding was to be seen in the circus ring, which was the theatre of operation for such experts as Baucher, James Fillis, and more recently Henri Cuyer. But present-day circus riding is seldom of a classical nature either in its production or execution, and it is the international competitors in World and European Dressage Championships and in the Olympic Games who, though amateur, are doing more than any other civilians to keep alive the art of classical equitation, as demonstrated in the performances of the best high school horses and riders.

Both the capriole *(above), a forward leap, and the* courbette *(right), a rear with hind legs straight, show a high level of training*

Work on two tracks is taken a stage further in high school riding than in intermediate dressage with full passes at the trot and the canter, both of which are extremely difficult for the horse, as they do require complete suppleness. Counter-changes on two tracks are harder still, with changes of direction from right to left lateral and vice versa, with the horse's bend to be altered smoothly every few strides. The ideal dispenses with the intervening stride for the horse to straighten, but causes the last stride in one direction to merge into the first stride in the other.

The Spanish Walk and the Spanish Trot, (which is not unlike *passage* except that the horse lifts each foreleg in turn and extends it fully in front of him at shoulder height and holds it horizontal for a split second before putting it down straight, without bending the knee), are spectacular movements but are not reckoned as being within the classical context by the purists. Because of this they are not included in Grand Prix dressage competitions. Though actually based on the action of pawing the ground, it is further contended that they are not natural movements and that the specific head carriage which they demand is injurious to the horse's collection and so jeopardises the rest of its training.

Chapter IV
History of Breeds

British pony breeds

THE world of ponies is going through a period of great activity at the moment. All the British native breeds are in demand all over the world and riding for children is now a popular and rewarding pastime.

What does the average family look for when it embarks upon the exciting purchase of a pony for the children? The most vital factor is the animal's temperament. A quiet sensible pony aids safety and reduces the risk of an accident, an all-important factor on the traffic-congested roads of today. Good conformation in the animal is also important: here the British are fortunate that their splendid pony breeds possess good bone structure, narrow withers and shapely hard hooves.

A novice about to embark upon the purchase of a pony will doubtless find the different breeds and their characteristics confusing, and will have much to learn before a success can be made of the venture. A pony is not like a bicycle which can be propped up against a wall and forgotten when the children have had their fun. It is a living creature demanding sustenance and shelter. Regular grooming is also essential. Its needs must be explored and considered before a decision to buy is finally taken.

It is extremely unwise for parents who intend to keep the pony out in a paddock all year round, to look at Thoroughbred ponies and to imagine that their children will soon be competing among the stars of the show ring. Blood ponies and championship rosettes are not for the novice. Much experience and hard work go into looking after these beautiful show ponies and training them and their young riders. Good looks are not so important as a willing, kind disposition which will contribute much more enjoyment and happiness. Riding a pony may be regarded as part of a child's education and it must be embarked upon with seriousness.

A discussion of the different pony breeds and the uses to which they may be put follows below. Not every pony you see will be a pure-bred native, but it is immensely valuable to study the right types.

The smallest of all pony breeds is the Shetland. These ponies are renowned for

These Welsh Mountain ponies, like other British breeds, are very hardy and are exported all over the world

Dartmoor and Exmoor ponies make reliable children's mounts, and because they are natural jumpers they make excellent gymkhana and hunting ponies. Not many children can expect to own a pony for each of these activities; these breeds are dual-purpose animals which will hunt in the winter and compete cheerfully and willingly at Pony Club functions during the summer months. They stand no higher than 12·2 hands; bay and brown are the preferred colours, but white markings, however insignificant, are discouraged.

A larger breed, popular for driving as well as for riding, is the New Forest pony which displays a free action, has good shoulders and head and makes a practical pony for teenage children; because it averages 13 to 14·2 hands in height. These ponies are admirable for hunting, being good jumpers and adept at getting across country, displaying a good turn of speed when required.

Ponies from Wales are among our most attractive breeds, and find great favour in the show ring. The breed divides into three distinct groups, the Welsh Mountain pony, the Welsh pony and the Welsh cob. Their exceptional good looks make them very popular, and because showing ponies at gymkhanas and shows has become popular, there are now more Welsh pony studs than any other breed in the British Isles. They have the proud head and tail carriage of the Arab, fine muzzles, dark eyes and a concave profile. They are fast and keen and must be carefully broken for

Left: Dales are good trotters and are often used to pull traps. Below: Shetland ponies are renowned for a combination of small stature and great strength

their miniature stature combined with great strength and hardiness. They grow profuse manes and tails, and thick heavy coats in winter. They may be dark brown, bay or black, although black predominates. The potential of the Shetland as a riding pony is necessarily limited by its size. Unfortunately the breed has also acquired an undeserved reputation for being unreliable and bad-tempered.

In fact, when properly schooled and managed, Shetlands make good ponies for the very young. In too many cases, however, they are expected to understand what is wanted of them without ever having been taught the rudiments and are just as frequently spoiled by being given too many titbits!

Exmoor and Dartmoor ponies are delightful, and are slightly larger than Shetlands. They have a strong 'pony' sense, which consists of a unique combination of sagacity and intelligence, and their supporters maintain that they are the hardiest of all the small pony breeds. Well-broken

Above: Dartmoor ponies make dependable jumpers and are much in demand

novice riders, but when this is done they display a wisdom and inherently kind temperament which make them delightful to own.

Connemara ponies originate in Ireland, are predominantly grey in colour and are very popular with older children and adults. They are much in demand for hunting and Pony Club work.

The Fell pony, chiefly seen in Northumberland, Cumberland and Westmorland, and the attractive Highland pony, remain to be discussed. These two breeds average 13·2 hands to 14 hands in height and are immensely strong and sturdy, being bred for hill work. The Highland pony is still used for transporting deer shot by stalkers in the highlands. Both breeds are docile and hardy and very popular as family ponies—for every member of the family can ride them as they are very well built and sturdy. Fell and Highland ponies predominate in the stables of pony-trekking centres as they are very sure-footed, and will trek all day with a free stride and at a steady pace.

Before venturing to buy a pony it is a good idea for the young prospective owner to visit the nearest reputable riding establishment and to enrol for a course of riding lessons. He or she must try to learn all that can be learned about ponies, although much will depend upon how much experienced help the parents can provide. It is certainly wise for the rider to know how to look after a pony before it arrives, as well as knowing how to ride it, rather than to leave these important matters until later.

The most satisfactory way to buy a pony is to purchase one from a family whose own children have outgrown it. This is not always possible because the genuine quiet ponies usually move from family to family without being advertised or taken to public sales. But children do outgrow their ponies, and parents today cannot afford to keep pets which are now idle, however much-loved they may be, so prospective buyers should keep their ears open and perhaps they may be lucky enough to hear of an outgrown pony.

It is important to try a pony before buying, to handle it in the stable and to make sure that it is easy to catch in the field. This last point is all-important, because it is extremely irritating to set aside an hour for riding and to have to spend most of that time, with other exasperated members of the family, pursuing the animal round its paddock before beginning to ride. Ponies that are not easily caught must be rejected.

Caution is advisable when buying at a public auction. A few good ponies are sold under the hammer, but there are pitfalls here for the inexperienced novice and there are more useless animals disposed of by auction than in any other way. A good child's pony does not often reach a public auction ring. A horse dealer is a man who sells horses and ponies for a livelihood. A well-established dealer, known in the neighbourhood, lives by his reputation and is, on the whole, a trustworthy character. The old belief that the dealer will sell a useless nag disguised as a good one is not strictly true today. If you buy from a dealer, take an experienced friend along to see the pony and arrange to have it on a week's trial. If the dealer agrees to this arrangement it is very likely to be a genuinely good pony, but it must be remembered that the dealer is under no obligation to allow a trial period. Be wary of advertisements in papers because they can be misleading. The animals are likely to be described in glowing terms but they are not always, in reality, all that they are described to be. Again, ask if you can have the pony on trial to discover its true worth and potential usefulness.

Below: Connemara ponies are very sure-footed and excellent jumpers

The Thoroughbred

THE evolution of the horse from the very earliest times, when the ancestors of our present equine species began to lose their toes and to walk upon a recognizable hoof, has been marked by numerous specific and significant developments. The early changes in form and habit between 3000 to 2000 BC, prior to the domestication of the horse, were dictated by environment and were part of a gradual process spreading over thousands of years. Thereafter, however, the evolutionary process accelerated as the human race, seeing the horse as a means of assisting its own progress, took an increasingly large part in the development of animals best suited for the purposes of transport, communication and, most particularly, of war.

Over the centuries that followed, the first recorded domestication was made of the horse by the Indo-European tribes which inhabited the steppe lands north of the mountain ranges bordering what we now know as the Black and Caspian Seas. Specific types of horses, selectively bred for one use or another, began to appear. The apotheosis was reached in the establishment of the warm-blood Oriental horse, which we call the Arab and which must be acknowledged as the foundation of the world's breeds, since there are few breeds, if any, that do not owe their existence to the prepotency of these desert-bred horses.

It was due to the importation of these Oriental horses into England during the eighteenth century, that the next great watershed in the development of the present-day riding horse was reached. This was the emergence of the English Thoroughbred, whose name is synonymous with the sport of racing.

Doctor Zhivago, with J. Docker in the saddle, winning the Players Gold Leaf Trophy at Newbury in 1973.

The exact origin of the world's premier breed of horses is a matter of some controversy and there are authorities who disagree with the late Lady Wentworth's positive and sweeping assertion that the Thoroughbred is entirely and exclusively the product of Arabian blood. Lady Wentworth (1873–1957) was possibly the greatest authority on the Arabian horse and her book, 'The Authentic Arabian Horse', is rightly considered to be the most comprehensive and important work on the subject, while her monumental study 'Thoroughbred Racing Stock' is of almost equal standing.

Racing and racehorses were an integral part of the English sporting scene for centuries before the formative period of the Thoroughbred, which took place during the hundred or so years following the Stuart Restoration in 1660. It would therefore be reasonable to assume that native horses already existed which, when crossed with the Arab, contributed to producing the combination of qualities characteristic of today's Thoroughbred.

This theory is based upon the belief that there was a well-established breed of native 'running horses' in Britain before the large importations of Oriental blood (known variously as Barb, Turk or Arabian) that took place in the latter part of the seventeenth century and continued well into the eighteenth. On the other hand, it is known that efforts were made to improve the native horses by the importation of both Oriental sires and mares well before that time. So it can be argued that the running horses might well have carried a proportion of Oriental blood. However, no concrete evidence is available. What is certain, however, is that James I had Arabians in his stud of race horses, among them the famous Markham Arabian.

Sir John Fenwick, Master of Horse to Charles II is said to have furthered the influx of Oriental blood by bringing back, at the command of his master, the 'Royal Mares', as well as some stallions, from the Levant. That, at any rate, is the explanation, given in the General Stud Book, of the Royal Mares found in so many early Thoroughbred pedigrees. It is more probable that these mares were supplied, from various sources, by James D'Arcy, Master of the Royal Stud, who had a contract with the King to supply 'twelve extraordinary good colts' each year for the royal stud at Sedbury, Yorkshire, for an annual payment of £800.

This Thoroughbred is a result of selective breeding with the Arabian

Nonetheless, during this period (1721 to 1759) some 200 Oriental horses are listed in Volume II of the General Stud Book. Of these, 176 were stallions, of whom three exerted a particular influence on the subsequent development of Thoroughbred stock. These were the Darley and Godolphin Arabians and the Byerley Turk, and all modern Thoroughbreds are descended from them in the male line.

The Darley Arabian was imported in 1705 by a Yorkshire squire, Mr Richard Darley. This dark bay horse came from a racing strain of desert-bred Arabians, the Managhi, and was a pure Kehilan (the word meaning 'Thoroughbred'). The Darley was the founder of the Eclipse line. Eclipse was the horse that inspired Dennis O'Kelly, it's owner, to make the remark, 'Eclipse first, the rest nowhere', and he was proved right, for it was never beaten up to the time it retired from the racecourse in 1760.

The Godolphin Arabian came to Britain in 1728 and lived to the ripe old age of 29, dying in 1753, in Cambridgeshire, on the Gogmagog estate of its owner Lord Godolphin. The Godolphin's origins are obscure but it is generally held that it was of the Jilfan strain from the Yemen and was one of four horses presented to the French King by the Bey of Tunis. It was subsequently bought by a Derbyshire landowner, Edward Coke.

The Godolphin founded the Matchem line. Matchem was foaled in 1748, being by the Godolphin's son, Cade. Although not so successful on the racecourse as its half-brother, Gimcrack, whose memory is perpetuated by the Gimcrack Stakes for two-year-olds held at York in August, Matchem was far more successful than the latter as a stallion.

The last of the 'founding fathers', the Byerley Turk, was, in fact, the first of the three to come to England. This stallion was captured from the Turks at the Battle of Buda in 1686 by Captain Robert Byerley and was ridden at the Battle of the Boyne. The Byerley Turk sired Jigg, which founded the Herod line from whence came the Tetrarch and other great horses of this century.

There were, of course, other Oriental stallions whose influence can still be seen, although not in the male top line. The Leedes Arabian, for instance, appears in

Nijinsky has the characteristic running qualities of the English Thoroughbred

more pedigrees than any other stallion and every grey Thoroughbred traces back to Alcock's Arabian.

Few, if any, of these stallions (and certainly not the three foundation sires) ever ran in a race. That poses the question why the breeders of the seventeenth and eighteenth centuries made so much use of horses that had not been subjected to the process of selection and rejection imposed by their performance on the racecourse. Certainly it was not because of the speed of the Arabian, which would have been of little account even in those days. The conclusion, therefore, is that the Arab was used because of its inherited quality and its ability to breed true to type, an essential in any breeding enterprise and particularly so in circumstances where the native stock has been debased.

In order to establish and improve a breed, it is imperative to keep reliable records of pedigrees and matings, as well as records of performance in the case of racehorses. Early records of the Thoroughbred are, naturally enough, not entirely comprehensive but, by 1791 when the first of Weatherby's General Stud Books appeared, a definite pattern had been established. Today's General Stud Book, still published by the same family, includes all pure-bred mares and their progeny, together with pedigrees of both mares and sires. Only animals entered in it are eligible to compete on licensed courses in Britain. Therefore, the English Thoroughbred can be defined as a horse of proven pedigree eligible for entry in the General Stud Book.

The word Thoroughbred, as applied to the racehorse, was not used until 1821 when it appeared in Volume II of Weatherby's General Stud Book and it was not until much later that Arabian outcrosses ceased and the English Thoroughbred was established as a breed in its own right. Indeed, it is only in the last 100 years that the Thoroughbred has increased so remarkably in numbers.

In 1962 the world Thoroughbred population, within the racing and breeding world, was estimated by Franco Varolo in the magazine *Courses et Elevages* as 233,000. Now, some ten years later, it is probably approaching more than 400,000. Of course, the Thoroughbred exists in quite large numbers outside racing.

That a near-perfect racing machine has evolved over such a comparatively short period, is a tribute to the knowledge, judgment and enthusiasm of the generations concerned with its production.

Apart from the necessary quality of speed, the Thoroughbred is the ideal riding horse. In movement, the action is long, low, free, easy and fast at all paces and since action is dependent upon conformation, that of the Thoroughbred is the nearest to perfection. Add to this the elusive factor of quality combined with balance, the true symmetry of proportions, and the Thoroughbred is without doubt the aristocrat of the equine species.

In all these respects it far exceeds its progenitor the Arab, yet it still retains the latter's fire and courage. Generations of confined breeding, however, combined with other factors, have resulted in a loss of much of the inherent soundness that is a characteristic of the Arab horse. This apart, the Thoroughbred is regarded as the ideal cross to produce hunters and jumpers when mated with half-bred mares, or indeed with Arabs and Arab crosses. It is also largely responsible for the unique and supremely elegant English riding pony–the latter emerging as a result of crossing Thoroughbreds with British native ponies, particularly the Welsh breeds.

Although the Thoroughbred evolved in England, the breed soon became established in other countries in large numbers. Today the largest Thoroughbred population is found in America which has the most highly capitalized racing industry in the world.

The first notable Thoroughbred exported to America was Bulle Rock who was claimed to be out of a mare by the Byerley Turk and sired by the Darley Arabian. He was followed by a number of notable stallions including Little Janus, a grandson of the Godolphin Arabian, who became a famous sire of fast horses. But these early horses, whose progeny up to the mid-nineteenth century competed in races decided by four-mile heats, have had little influence on the modern American Thoroughbred which has been developed deliberately to race very fast over a limited distance at an early age.

It was, indeed, long after the War of Independence that the American Thoroughbred received a significant stimulus from such horses as Medley, which was by Gimcrack, and Diomed, a son of Florizel who was by Herod. Medley proved to be a sire of brood mares which when put to Diomed had a lasting effect on the evolution of the American racehorse.

Diomed was the sire of Sir Archie, who was probably the best son of this remarkable horse. Sir Archie was as successful at stud as on the track. Boston, a male line descendant of Diomed and Sir Archie, was the leading sire between 1851 and 1853 and his sons, Lexington and Lecomte, were conceived during his last stud season.

Lexington was one of America's great sires, leading the table in no less than sixteen seasons, and his descendants filled the stud book by the end of the nineteenth century when a fixed type of American horse had become apparent. Such a situation, however, demanded the import of fresh blood if progress was to continue. Of these imports the most important were Leamington, Glencoe, Australian and Eclipse (which was by Orlando and should not be confused with either the original Eclipse or the American Eclipse).

The Civil War was the dividing line which marked the change in emphasis and character of American racing. Long distance heats were replaced by short races of from five furlongs to a mile and a half and racing became a popular entertainment. Its popularity increased still further when betting was introduced. The era produced Iroquois, by Leamington, owned by Pierre Lorillard. Iroquois won the English Derby in 1881, was second in the 2000 Guineas and won the St. Leger. The international American Thoroughbred had arrived and the situation was confirmed when Foxall, a son of Lexington, went to France to win the Grand Prix de Paris and then won the Cesarewitch, the Cambridgeshire and, in the year following, the Ascot Gold Cup. Thereafter American horses figured prominently on the English and French tracks despite a depression in American racing. This was the result of the New York law of 1910 which prohibited betting and the Jersey Act of 1913. This act was set up by the Earl of Jersey, who was a steward of the Jockey Club. The act stated that only horses whose ancestors could be traced to horses in previous volumes of the *General Stud Book* would be admitted to it thereafter. A similar policy was adopted in France and this prevented the majority of North American Thoroughbreds from being exported to Britain and France. American Strains that were already included in the stud book however, were not expunged. After World War II, the French had many spectacular wins in England with horses that had American strains in their ancestry. This brought about a change of attitude to American Thoroughbreds and in 1948 the ban was removed.

In the meantime America's greatest racehorse appeared on the scene. This was Man O'War, bred in 1917 by Mahubah, a son of Rock Sand, winner of the English Triple Crown in 1903, and winner of all but one of his 21 races. Man O'War figures in the pedigrees of numerous top-class horses, Buckpasser and Arts and Letters on the American tracks, for instance, and Derby winners like Never Say Die, Relko and Sir Ivor in the international field.

Further impetus was given by the importation from France of Teddy and his sons Sir Galahad III and Bull Dog. These were followed by the valuable additions of the Aga Khan's stallions, the three Derby winners Blenheim, Mahmoud and Bahram and by Hyperion's sons Alibhai, Khaled and the brilliant Nasrullah, the latter creating an enormous impact on American breeding. Bold Ruler, the epitome of the American Thoroughbred, was one of his sons.

Thereafter the American success story, backed by heavy capitalisation, was assured still further by the French Sea Bird, winner of the Derby, and the Italian Ribot, both of whom went to the USA on five-year leases.

Since then, American-bred horses have proved consistently the strength of the racing industry in the USA, taking as much as their fair share, and sometimes more, in the battle between the leading racing nations, America, France, England and Ireland.

Left and Right: Secretariat is just one of the many superb Thoroughbreds which has resulted from the American racing industry in recent years

The Arab

THE origin of the Arab horse is a complex mixture of legend, fact and surmise, but there is no doubt that this is the oldest of the world's recognized breeds and that the influence of the Arab on the world horse population is greater than that of any other horse.

Just when the Arab breed became established can never be proven, and experts disagree about the assertion of the late Lady Wentworth who stated categorically that the breed existed in pure form as long ago as 5,000 BC. She clearly regarded the Arab as a separate creation, but today that belief is rarely held.

The Arab historian El Kelbi (786 AD) traced the pedigrees of Arabian horses from the time of Baz, great-great-grandson of Noah, who captured and tamed the wild horses of the Yemen. El Kelbi's feat was, in fact, unusual for an Arab, a race that rarely kept written records. His pedigrees show a line of descent from a stallion, Hoshaba, and a mare called Baz. There is evidence on Egyptian monuments, dated about 1,300 BC, of horses of recognizable Arabian type, and it was in Egypt that the first representation of a ridden horse was found, a statuette from about 2,000 BC, showing a very Arab-like horse. These same types occur again in the rock carvings of Nejd and Syria. Writing in the eighteenth century, the Emir Abd-el-Kader (1808–1883) divided the history of the Arabian into four eras, Adam to Ishmael, Ishmael to Solomon, Solomon to Mohammed, and Mohammed onwards. Since the Semitic Arabs did not exist as a people in the days of Adam, the first division is not entirely relevant. But with Ishmael, who was the personification of the Arab desert dweller, we can perceive the first close association between these nomads and what was to become known throughout the world as the Arab horse.

Ishmael was an outcast, banished to the harsh and inhospitable desert lands. We learn in the Bible of the angel who spoke to Ishmael's mother Hagar, saying 'He shall be a fierce man. He shall lift his hand against all men and they shall lift their hands against him.' In order to survive, Ishmael had to depend upon his swift war horses, the necessary accompaniment of the raiding and pillage which was his way of life.

With the death of Ishmael the tribes dispersed and, without the stimulus provided by constant warfare, the horses

The Arabian is probably the most famous of all the horse breeds, noted for its beauty, elegance and docile temperament. This magnificent Arab stallion (below) and mare and foal (right) show the distinctive dished face, typical of the Arab

began to degenerate. It was then the turn of Solomon to maintain the Arab breed, which he did to some effect by keeping 1,200 saddle horses and 40,000 chariot horses in his stables.

The last era is, however, the most significant in the development of the Arab horse. Because of Mohammed, who was a soldier, religious leader and astute politician, the faith of Islam spread far beyond its desert boundaries. The Muslim cavalry, long after the death of its Prophet, conquered Egypt and North Africa and penetrated through Spain and France. These conquerors took with them their horses, now much up-graded, since their care and development had become an article of the faith, incorporated deep in the heart of Muslim life. It is from this point that the superlative breed of horses, created by the stimulus of religious observance, was brought into contact with horses of the conquered lands and the extraordinary influence of the Arab horse on the world's equine development began.

At first the Arab was mainly used in England for the development of the racing Thoroughbred. Breeding Arabian horses did not begin seriously until the latter half of the nineteenth century, when the Crabbet Park Arabian Stud was founded by Sir Wilfred and Lady Anne Blunt. It was carried on by their daughter, Lady Wentworth, and is still one of the leading Arab studs in Britain. In Europe, Poland was once a leading Arab-breeding country. The Chrestowka Stud, which was devoted mainly to Arabs, was established in 1508. Unfortunately all their bloodlines were destroyed during the two World Wars, and breeders had to start again with imported stock. Arabs are bred very extensively in the USA. The Midwest is a great centre for Arab-breeding, despite the inhospitable climate.

Almost every breed known in the world today owes something to the prepotency of Arab blood, but the breed's greatest achievement is as the progenitor of the world's fastest and most valuable horse, the English Thoroughbred. The Thoroughbred was developed in England in the late seventeenth and early eighteenth centuries largely from three imported Arab sires: the Byerley Turk (Turk, Barb, and Arabian tended to be synonymous names at the time), the Darley Arabian and the famous Godolphin Arabian, which was originally called El Sham when presented as a gift to the French king. The horse, however, did not find royal favour and before coming to England in 1728 pulled a cart round the Paris streets. The Godolphin died in 1753 at the age of 39 years, having founded the Matchem line of the English Thoroughbred.

The Byerley Turk was brought to England by Captain Robert Byerley in 1680 and was ridden by him at the Battle of the Boyne in the following year. The Byerley is responsible for establishing the Herod line.

The Darley Arabian, imported in 1705 by a Yorkshire squire, Richard Darley, is probably the most important of the

This beautiful grey Moroccan Arab is decked out in Bedouin trappings, looking very much the same as its ancestors did when they were ridden into battle

three and founded the line of the great racehorse, Eclipse. This horse was a Kehilan (pure-bred) of the Managli racing strain prized by the Anazeh Arabs. It is held that there are five superlative strains of Arab horse, an aristocracy known as the Khamsa, from which stem all the hundreds of sub-strains. These are the Kehilan (pure- or thorough-bred), a strain often termed Kehilan-Ajuz, after the greatest of Arabian mares, Ajuz, a name meaning both ancient and noble; Seglawi (the pure strain now being Seglawi Jedran); Abeyan; Hadban (not so numerous); and Hamdani. This last is the strain most likely to produce greys which are not–contrary to popular opinion–a predominant Arab colour. The lesser-known Alcock Arabian was of the Hamdani strain and appears in the pedigree of every grey Thoroughbred–a remarkable example of prepotency.

Most of the British pony breeds owe something, and in some cases (such as that of the Welsh Mountain pony) a great deal, to Arab blood. Elsewhere the influence is equally marked and generally acknowledged. In France there is the Anglo-Arab, containing a minimum of 25 per cent Arab blood in relation to that of Thoroughbred. The Percheron and Boulonnais have Arab blood, and the Normandy saddle horse, too. Most European breeds, in fact, as well as those of Asia and nearly all American ones, contain Arabian elements.

The unique position occupied by the Arabian horse is based, broadly, on three factors: first, to its antiquity as a breed of fixed type and character; secondly, to the development and improvement effected over centuries in its original environment and, finally, as a result of these two, the Arabian supremacy is due to the inherent qualities of soundness, conformation, courage and speed with which the Arab stamps its stock indelibly and consistently.

The present-day Arab remains as distinctive as ever and those of the highest class are still small in comparison with the Thoroughbred. A horse between 14·2 hh and 15 hh is regarded as being the most true to type, although there are bigger pure-breds than these.

The finely drawn head with its pronouncedly 'dished' face and the large widely spaced eyes are typical, as are the large, flared nostrils, the tapered muzzle and the shapely ears. The Arab has several significant characteristics which set it apart from other breeds. It has five lumbar vertebrae instead of the normal six and its tail has 16 instead of 18 vertebrae, and this contributes to the gay elevated carriage of the tail. The shaft of the ulna (elbow joint) is complete, not vestigial as in other breeds of horse.

Blue Arabian horses have become so highly prized in America that they have a separate breed register, known as The Blue Arabian Horse Catalog

Because the Arab structure differs from others in the number of ribs and lumbar bones, the back and quarters are of unmistakable formation. The back is short but very strong and carried on an almost level croup. The tail is arched and, when the horse is in motion, is carried like a banner. The hair of both tail and mane is silky in texture. In other respects the Arab conforms to the desirable points of conformation applicable to any horse, but it has to be confessed that some Arabs are not as good in the hind leg as they should be–a fault to be avoided in breeding. But above all, the Arab is supremely refined and beautiful, full of fire and courage, yet infinitely gentle.

Today, the Arab is bred in every country where horses exist and retains all its old characteristics. It is not, of course, nearly so fast as the Thoroughbred, nor are many pure-breds seen in show jumping competitions and three-day events, although Arabs can and do jump. It remains, however, the supreme horse for endurance riding because of its soundness and stamina, qualities which are not surpassed by any other breed. Furthermore, it has to be remembered that all horses in competitive sport derive from the Arab to a greater or lesser degree and that, outside of Thoroughbred breeding, it continues to play an essential part in the development and up-grading of other breeds.

In Great Britain, the interests of the Arab are catered for by the Arab Horse Society, which was set up in 1918 with the object of preserving the pure Arab blood which already existed. It has issued eight volumes of the Arab Stud Book and also issues an Anglo-Arab and Part-bred Arab register. Pure-bred Arabs are also included in the General Stud Book.

The Anglo-Arab horse

THE Anglo-Arab, as its name implies, is the product of the Arab and the Thoroughbred, the latter, of course, deriving in part from Arabian blood. In the strictest sense the Anglo-Arab horse cannot be regarded as a 'pure' breed, since new blood, either Arab or Thoroughbred, is continually being added. Nevertheless, it is recognized throughout the world as being an 'established' breed, having its own well-defined characteristics. In France it is accorded its own stud book.

The fusion of the world's two premier breeds should, in theory, and frequently does in practice, produce a riding horse which combines the finest qualities of both, while at the same time avoiding their faults. One disadvantage of the modern Thoroughbred, for example, is that it is not always temperamentally suited to the tasks it is required to perform. Often it tends to be too excitable and impetuous for the disciplines involved in dressage training or for the precision needed in the show jumping arenas. Moreover, the Thoroughbred cannot be said to have retained the inherent soundness of its ancestor, the Arab.

Where the Thoroughbred scores decisively over the much smaller pure-bred Arabian horse is in speed and jumping ability. The Anglo-Arab has inherited these qualities as well as the Thoroughbred's natural balance and good riding conformation, and from the Arab it has derived intelligence, soundness and stamina. The result is a riding horse of the finest type, even if it is not as fast as the Thoroughbred.

In Britain, the Arab Horse Society maintains three stud books: for Arabs, Anglo-Arabs and part-bred Arabs. To qualify for inclusion in the Anglo-Arab book, a horse must be able to claim not less than 12½ per cent Arab blood. Since the establishment of the English Thoroughbred as a distinct breed during the nineteenth century (from the point when recrossing to the pure Arab ceased), there have been numerous examples of English Anglo-Arabs that have proved their excellence in every equestrian field outside the racecourse. Anglo-Arabs have their special classes at the annual Arab Horse Show and classes are provided for them at a number of shows in Great Britain.

This handsome Anglo-Arab horse comes from France

In recent years Anglo-Arabs have been successful in show hack classes, as dressage, show jumping and event horses, and also as hunters. Nonetheless, the development of the Anglo-Arab in Britain is insignificant when compared with the standing attained by the Anglo-Arab in France. The pre-eminence of the French Anglo-Arab is due to the encouragement given to its breeding by the long-established state-owned national studs which have influenced horse breeding in France since they were created in the seventeenth century by Louis XIV's Minister of Finance, Colbert.

No such situation has ever existed in Britain, where horse breeding is, and has always been, in the hands of a number of individuals, usually operating on a comparatively small scale. It is true, of course, that breed societies are extremely active in this country but membership, although necessary, is voluntary. There is no official body which can arbitrarily control the breeding of horses. The only governing factors are the conditions of registration in the stud book of each breed, and the definitions of type and characteristics which are laid down for guidance.

In France, Colbert's early national studs served mainly as a source of supply for the Royal Stables and it was not until the arrival of the Emperor Napoleon I, that the studs began to take the form that they have today.

The home of the French Anglo-Arab is in the south-west of France at the studs of Pompadour, Tarbes, Gelos and Pau. A race of horses existed in this part of France in ancient times and was known to the Romans as the race of Aquitaine, and then at various times as the race of Bigorre, of Navarre and as the Meridian Half-bred. This native breed received infusions from the horses of Barbarian invaders, possibly of some unknown Eastern strain, and, at a later date, an influx of Oriental blood from the cavalry horses left behind by the Moors, after their defeat at Poitiers in AD 720 and their subsequent retreat beyond the Pyrenees.

Napoleon, increasingly wasteful in his

use of horses and of men, was in constant need of cavalry replacements for his ambitious campaigns. He favoured the small, tough Arabs for use as his personal chargers and realized that a crossing of Arab blood with the horses already existing in the south-west of France would produce ideal cavalry remounts. As a result, the stud known as the Haras National de Tarbes was founded in 1806, together with the studs of Pompadour and Pau.

The English Thoroughbred element was introduced around 1830 when 'English blood', adding size and speed, became fashionable in France. Initially the French were over-enthusiastic, using so much Thoroughbred blood that the original qualities desirable in a cavalry horse–hardiness, stamina and a level head–were lost. However, the lesson was learned and breeders of later generations practised a rigorous system of Thoroughbred selection, based on performance, stamina and conformation, that has persisted to this day.

The modern French Anglo-Arab can be the product of three elements: Anglo-Arab, Arab and Thoroughbred. The dam may be any one of these so long as the progeny possesses 25 per cent Arab blood, the minimum for inclusion in the French Anglo-Arab stud book. A number of permutations is therefore possible in the production of eligible progeny.

The French Anglo-Arab, subject to the academic reservation made at the opening of this article, must be regarded now as being a definite breed, and far more so than its English counterpart. Pedigrees, indeed, usually show either one or both parents to be Anglo-Arabs. It is noteworthy that the best products of the French studs show between the minimum 25 per cent and 45 per cent Arab blood, and that many of the Olympic medals gained by France in the equestrian events, as well as the numerous honours in international show jumping, have been achieved by such Anglo-Arabs.

It is the practice to mate an Arab stallion to a Thoroughbred mare, but few of the pure-bred Arabs used as stallions are bred at the national studs. It is thought preferable to import these from Syria, and in particular from Tunisia, where climate and soil conditions encourage the necessary and much-prized hardiness and the old Arabian character.

The Anglo-Arab, though not a pure breed, has stamina, courage and speed

As an additional and most important factor in the breeding of the French Anglo-Arab, the racing programme confined to the breed provides an excellent means of selection or rejection according to performance.

The present-day Anglo-Arab is usually about 16 hands high and rarely exceeds 16.2 or 16.3 hh. Its conformation is marked by well-set and clearly defined withers, sloping shoulders, roomy girth, good limbs and joints and excellent, hard feet. Endowed with intelligence, sobriety, endurance, balance, weight-carrying capacity and of speed, this is one of the world's greatest all-round riding horses.

Horses of the Orient

IT is to the hot-blooded (that is, thoroughbred) Oriental horse, typified by the Arabian, that the world owes the existence of the light horse breeds that we know today. It would, however, be a mistake to consider the horses of the Orient solely in terms of the Arabian.

Mongolia, for instance, has every right to be considered as the earliest centre of evolution and is still the home, in the area of the Takin Shar Nuru (the Yellow Horse Mountains) of the only surviving species of wild horse, known as Przewalski's horse (*Equus Przewalskii*), from which the present-day Mongolian pony descends, as well as many other Eastern types and breeds.

It can, indeed, be argued with justification that to this Asiatic horse and to the near-extinct Tarpan, which until the end of the last century was distributed fairly widely over southern European Russia and eastern Europe, may be credited at least the part-origin of the Arabian and other Oriental breeds.

Przewalski's horse is today much the same as it was in the Ice Age. This breed derives its name from the Russian explorer, Colonel Nicolai Przewalski, who discovered specimens on the borders of the Gobi Desert. Unfortunately, the breed's survival is being threatened increasingly by the encroachment of civilization on its traditional territory. However, there are over 140 specimens in the great zoos of Europe and North America. It stands between 12 and 14 hh and is of dun colouring ranging from cream to red. Usually zebra stripes are apparent on the limbs and there is a notable dorsal stripe. The mane is characteristically upright and the tail sparse. Its qualities of speed and endurance, so essential in its hostile environment, have also been preserved through the generations.

Left: Equus Przewalskii; this wild horse is the same today as it was in the Ice Age. Below: a Mongolian horse

Nor has its descendant, the Mongolian pony, changed so very much from the pony which carried the hordes of Genghis Khan from their homeland in the Gobi Desert to rage through the known world of their day and to reach, in 1240 AD, right into the Carpathians. Of all the world's horses it is unlikely that there are any that approach the Mongol pony in stamina and toughness. They survive, and even thrive, on the poorest feeding and are yet fleet of foot over short distances and can endure journeys so long that they are beyond the comprehension of the European horseman. Indeed, Scott made his attempt to reach the South Pole (1912–13) on very similar ponies. They are found in the states of Inner and Outer Mongolia, between Manchuria to the east, Turkestan to the west, Siberia to the north, and Tibet and China to the south.

These ponies are between 12.2 and 13 hh and there is considerable variation in conformation. Most, however, have coarse, long and heavy heads and a generally primitive quality, but they are otherwise thick-set and muscular. They have well-sprung ribs, strong quarters, good bone and iron-hard feet. They are used extensively for riding, draught and pack work, they represent a supply of meat on the hoof and the mares are milked after foaling for some three months – a very economic, all-purpose animal. The breed has been improved in recent years by the introduction of Thoroughbred, Arab and other foreign blood.

China has, in fact, as many as seven major types of pony and six local breeds, most being based on the Mongolian. To China, also, must go the distinction of being the only great power to maintain a significant cavalry force. There are no less than three divisions whose job is to patrol the troublesome Western frontier where the rough ground prohibits any other form of transport than these Mongolian ponies.

Ponies, indeed, are numerous throughout the East, although in general they are

Above: ponies of eastern Indonesia and Timor often have Arab blood. Left: a horse native to Afghanistan

poor specimens in appearance when compared with the beautiful animals to be found in Europe.

In Indonesia, for example, where the pony plays an important part in the economy, there are a number of pony breeds. The dun Sumba is very much a primitive type and is famous for its dancing ability, the owners teaching the ponies, which are decorated with knee bells, to dance to the rhythm of tom-toms. A pony with more quality and showing marked Arab characteristics is the Sandalwood, which is raced and is regarded as being the most valuable of the Indonesian breeds. The Java is not so pretty and is usually cow-hocked, but nonetheless gets through an enormous amount of work pulling the two-wheeled 'sados', loaded to the limit, under the extremes of tropical heat. The island of Timor, which is an island of the East Indian Archipelago, south of the Banda Sea and north of Western Australia, has its own diminutive 'cow' pony of about 12 hh. This pony is used by the local cowboys who, like their Western counterparts, catch cattle with a lasso. Sumatra, too, has its own breed, the Batak, which is now carefully bred and has benefited from Arab importations.

When the ponies came to Indonesia is not known, but since many resemble the Mongolians it is possible that they came in ancient times with the Chinese. It is interesting to note that when ridden the ponies are fitted with bitless bridles similar to ones used 4,000 years ago in Asia.

To the Mongolian horse, which can be regarded as being nearer to the 'original' horse than any other, can also be attributed the Indian breeds, especially the Bhutan, Yarkand and Spiti of India's northern states, all of which originated from the ponies of Genghis Khan's hordes, which were left in camps along his line of communication north of Karakoram and Pamirs. The Burma pony, bred in the Shan Hills and used for pack work, and the strong little Manifpuri, on whom the British officers learnt their polo, are possibly also of the same origin.

The Arab, of course, has had an enormous influence on the Indian breeds, particularly the curved-eared Kathiawari and the hardy Marwari. The most notable importation to India, after the Arab, was, however, the Australian Waler, a predominantly Thoroughbred horse, which was brought into the country in large numbers to be used as a cavalry remount between the years of 1850 and 1930.

Finally, in any discussion of the horses of the Orient the Persian breeds cannot be omitted, since their influence is considerable and they must be classed as truly Oriental. Indeed, the Persians lay claim to having owned the forefathers of the Arab horse and today the Persian Arab is noted for its purity and absence of foreign (that is, non-Persian) blood. The Plateau Persian horse, a composite term covering a variety of horses of pronounced Eastern type, encompasses the Persian strains of Jaf, Basseri and Darashouri and, of course, the famed Turkmene, the racing horse which so closely resembles the Munighi Arabian, a strain that helped in the formation of the English Thoroughbred.

The Turkmene, noted for its speed as long ago as 1,000 BC, formed the Bactrian cavalry of the Persian King Darius. From this breed comes the golden Akhal-Teké, a horse of extraordinary stamina. It was the Turkmene, descended, it is said, from Bucephalus, the charger of Alexander the Great, that became known as the Heavenly Horse or the 'blood-sweating breed'. In order to acquire them, the rulers of ancient China found it necessary to make war in the two centuries preceding the birth of Christ.

The Turkmene is found in two distinct colours: bay and brown, with white markings and a golden tint, or grey, black and dun tinted with silver. The average height is 15.2 hh.

The endurance of this ancient breed is phenomenal. It is not as fast as the Thoroughbred, of which some authorities claim it could have been a part-progenitor rather than the Munighi Arabian, but few horses, Thoroughbred or otherwise, could equal one record accorded to a horse of this breed in 1935. In that year a Turkmene covered the distance between Ashabad and Moscow, which is some 4,300 kilometres, in only 84 days. This was a speed of almost 50 miles a day, which was a prodigious feat to maintain day in, day out for nearly three months.

Below: a shepherd boy on a Mongolian horse, which is descended from Equus Przewalskii

The horses of Europe

INITIALLY, world distribution of the horse population and its subsequent development was governed largely by the basic factors of climate, soil conditions, food availability and so on. Later, after domestication and selective breeding by man, and the development of the species was influenced still further as the horse was raised to serve specific purposes. Generally speaking, animals living in cold northern climates with sparse vegetation on which to feed, were small in size and grew thick coats as protection against the rigours of the winter weather. Conversely, in hot climates a finer animal, thin-skinned and of much greater quality, was produced. This was the 'hot-blooded' horse, which, in general terms, experts refer to as the Oriental horse.

Early in the history of the horse, the basic situation, in which horses and ponies were products of their environment, was as true of the continent of Europe as of anywhere else in the world. The horses of modern Europe, however, were for centuries subjected to the continued introduction of Oriental blood and, finally, of Thoroughbred blood. Over a period of time this resulted in the evolution of many clearly defined and fixed breeds–'warm-bloods'–owing little to environment and almost everything to man's urge to improve the animals over which he had dominion. Otherwise, of course, there remain in Europe many ancient breeds that retain their original environment-imposed characteristics, despite in some cases having been interbred with 'warm-blood' breeds; this is particularly true of the pony breeds and of some of the 'cold-blood' (phlegmatic) heavy draught horses.

As far as the horse is concerned, if not for its masters, national barriers in modern Europe are tending to disappear. For many years the Thoroughbred has been virtually an international breed, despite the fact that it originated in England. The same is true of the Arab, a breed that today is found in far greater numbers in countries outside the breed's original habitat. There are in Europe, for instance, English, Polish, Hungarian, French and Russian Arabs, and a good many more. All these are most definitely recognizable as belonging to one breed but, demonstrating that environment is still able to exert an influence, there is a subtle but, nonetheless, discernible variation in type. To a lesser degree, native ponies of the British Isles, in particular the Welsh, have been exported to a number of European countries and studs have been established in the Netherlands, Belgium, Germany and France.

Some years ago, Russian horses, of various breeds, were imported to England in fairly large numbers. They failed to make any significant mark on the English horse population, but there is no reason to suppose that an increasing interchange of horses will not continue among other European contries. English and Irish-bred horses, for example, are in demand all over Europe as event horses, while the Italian show jumpers are mounted almost exclusively on animals purchased in Ireland. Germany has, in the Hanoverian, a breed that is much in demand as a show jumper and a dressage horse. Nevertheless, despite the blurring of the equine frontiers, certain breeds, even though they may be found in considerable numbers elsewhere, remain jealously preserved in their traditional breeding areas.

Above: the Tarpan from Poland, Europe's wild and primitive dorsal-striped pony. Facing page: the domesticated Haflinger

The British Isles has always been noted for the quality of its horses and has a variety of breeds probably not exceeded by any country other than the USSR. The Thoroughbred was an English product bred from imported Arabians in the seventeenth and eighteenth centuries. From the Thoroughbred has evolved, in England and in Ireland, the hunter, which is not a breed, of course, but a very pronounced type. Britain's greatest assets, however, are her native ponies, bred for centuries on mountain and moorland, and the riding pony crosses obtained from them. The larger breeds are the Highland, Dale, Fell, Welsh Cob, Connemara and New Forest. The first four are of enormous strength in proportion to their size and the last two are perhaps more elegant, but all are good riding horses for either an adult or a child. The largest of them is the Welsh Cob, which may stand as high as 15 hh, whereas the others are unlikely to be over 14 hh. The smaller ponies are the tiny Shetland, the Exmoor, Dartmoor and the Welsh Mountain, the latter being possibly the most beautiful of them all with its Arab-like head.

Another breed native to Britain is the Cleveland Bay, a superb carriage horse from Yorkshire, which produces wonderful heavyweight hunters when crossed with the Thoroughbred. The Hackney, descended from the old Norfolk Roadsters, is the most spectacular of harness horses and ponies, and also belongs to Britain.

Ponies, of course, breed elsewhere in Europe. Poland, for instance, has quite a number, including a few specimens descended from the wild and primitive Tarpan (*Equus przewalskii gmelini*). No one could call these dorsal-striped ponies beautiful but, of course, they are of considerable historical interest. The nearest domesticated relatives to the Tarpan are the Konik and Huzul ponies, but neither of these breeds can compare in quality with the British ponies. This, in fact, is true of the majority of ponies existing on the Continent, where there has never existed, as in Britain, the large demand for a good, well-shaped pony. Germany has one semi-wild pony, the Dülmen. Norway has the strong Fjord, which is tough and resembles the Highland; the Northlands, belonging to the Baltic group of ponies; and the 'cold-blood' Dole-Gudbrandsal, resembling the Fell pony of Britain. From this last breed comes the Dole Trotter, produced by the introduction of trotting sires. The ponies of Greece are working horses but are essentially of Oriental origin, the best being the Peneia and Pindos ponies, and the worst, the Tarpan-type Skyros, found on the island of that name.

Best known of the continental ponies is the golden Haflinger of Austria, a number of which have come to Britain in recent years. Bred in the South Tyrol and Bavaria, it is a good all-purpose mountain pony, very strong but extremely willing and tractable.

The variety of continental 'warm-blood' horses is, of course, much greater. Poland, in the main, relies on the spirited, tough Arab that has been bred there since the late sixteenth century. There is also the more than useful Poznan horse, the best of which – those with the most Thoroughbred blood – make good middle-weight hunters. The Poznan is the result of improving local stock by the use of Arab, Thoroughbred and Masuren blood. This last breed is in fact the East Prussian horse, as renamed by the Poles. The Germans left a number of these horses behind when they left Poland in 1945 and the Poles incorporated them into their own breeding programmes.

The East Prussian, or Trakehner, is, in fact, one of Germany's most valuable breeds, although breeding was badly disrupted during the Second World War and many leading blood lines were destroyed. Trakehners make excellent saddle horses and are good jumpers. Possibly because of its success in the show jumping arenas, the big Hanoverian (formerly a carriage horse) is the best known of the German breeds. The increased use of Thoroughbred blood has added to the scope of the Hanoverian, and resulted in a somewhat lighter horse that excels at show jumping and has an extremely good temperament as a dressage horse. Similar to the Hanoverian is the Oldenburg, usually considered as a cavalry or harness type of horse. These horses are even bigger than the Hanoverians and the breed owes much to the Thoroughbred and Anglo-Arab. Of the same calibre is the Holstein, one of the oldest 'warm-bloods', which was bred from the war-horse of the Middle Ages and improved by the addition of Oriental and Spanish blood.

Hungary is a land of horses and horsemen, and ideally suited to the purpose of raising stock. Much emphasis is given to the Arab (locally known as the Shagya strain), and also to the Lipizzaner, which the Hungarians use mainly as a carriage horse. Hungary's own breeds are the Nonius and the Furioso. The latter is descended from the nineteenth-century Thoroughbred, Furioso, and the Norfolk Roadster, North Star. Later in the same century more Thoroughbred blood was introduced, including that of Vibar, son of Buccaneer, winner of the 1892 Ascot Gold Cup. Both the Nonius and Furioso

The small size of these Iceland ponies is a reflection of their poor environment

are active dual-purpose horses, being used under saddle and in harness.

One of the world's great horses, whose blood has had an influence (at least up to the time that the Thoroughbred became established) second only to that of the Arabian, is Spain's Andalusian, the parade horse of the Middle Ages and the mount of kings. Derived from the Barb, or Berber (the horse of the Moorish invaders of Spain, which was crossed with local stock), the Andalusian, or Spanish horse, is responsible for the Lipizzaner of Austria, Hungary and Yugoslavia, and for Czechoslovakia's Kladruber. The true Kladruber has almost disappeared, unfortunately, and a great deal of outside blood (Oldenburg, Hanoverian and Anglo-Norman) has been introduced. Among other horses that, to a greater or lesser extent, carry Andalusian blood, are two Danish breeds – the Frederiksburg and the spotted Knabstrup, descended from the spotted mare Flaebehoppen. In all probability, a number of British breeds such as the Cleveland, the Connemara and perhaps the Welsh contain Andalusian blood.

Italy is hardly a horse-breeding country today, but the Salerno (Salernitano) is bred in the area north of Rome, and there is also the Calabrese of Calabria. Both are good all-round riding horses and the former retains elements of the old Neapolitan blood. As a draught or pack horse Italy has the Avelignese, the Italian version of the Haflinger, and similarly descended.

France, on the other hand, apart from its superb Anglo-Arabs, has its Norman and Anglo-Norman horses, the Demi-Sang trotting horses, the Noram Trotter and the hardy, if otherwise much overrated, Camargue pony.

Perhaps one of the most famous trotters is the Russian Orlov, one of the most interesting of the many breeds from the USSR. The Orlov was evolved around 1777 by Count Alexis Orlov, who crossed judiciously the blood of Arabs, Thoroughbreds, Dutch, Mecklenburg and Danish. The Orlov was the supreme European trotter until the establishment in Europe of the American Trotter. The USSR also has the golden Turkmene, an ancient Oriental breed descended from the Bactrian horses that formed the cavalry of King Darius of Persia. Similar in appearance and descended from a Turkmene strain is the tough-constitutioned Akhal-Teké, a breed that paces naturally. Then there is the Don, fundamentally a steppe horse, tough and hard.

Throughout Europe there still exist the cold-blooded, heavy horses; the Belgian, Swedish and French Ardennes, the Schleswig, Rhineland and Jutland. In France there are the Breton, Percheron, Boulonnais and Poitevine; in Britain the descendants of the Great Horses, the Shires, the Clydesdales and the round-barrelled Suffolk Punch.

In most countries of Europe, the breeding of horses is largely under state control. In Britain, however, breeding is left in the hands of the individual, guided by breed societies that are under no obligation to any central government department or official body.

These Trakheners from East Prussia make excellent riding horses or show jumpers

Horses of the Camargue

BETWEEN the sea, the Rhône and the ancient town of Aigues-Mortes in the south of France, lies the harsh, inhospitable, wild land of the Camargue. There the hot, fierce sun bakes the ground until it cracks. In the winter nature covers this forbidding region with a sheet of salt water. The salt is everywhere, carried by the tearing wind, the *mistral*, which bends the stunted shrub growth and dries the faces of the men and women who live there to the consistency of parched leather. These people, nevertheless, still retain a fierce sense of pride in this swampland of the Rhône delta where they were born. They call it 'the most noble conquered territory of man' and they take pride in the fact that it is not easily subdued.

Ordinary men, bred to the softer comforts provided by better favoured parts of the world, are in some way powerfully attracted to the earth's desert places. It was so with the sandy wastes of Arabia before the Bedouin abandoned his desert horse for a Cadillac and an oil-well. It still holds good for the Camargue, which will doubtless soon be overrun by tourists, even if not defaced to the same extent by the material symbols of wealth.

Were it not for the tourist, however, it is questionable whether one romantic aspect of the Camargue would survive.

For among the principal attractions of the region are its celebrated white horses, the 'horses of the sea'. It is owing partly to tourist appeal and partly to the enthusiasm of a small number of horse-lovers that the breed of the Camargue still exists, and in a world where nature is all too often sacrificed to the interests of 'progress', one should be grateful that the *manades*, the herds of white horses, still inhabit the poor country which is their heritage.

In fact, the legendary white horses of the Camargue are not all that romantic, and they are certainly anything but beautiful with their large, square, straight heads, short necks and poor, upright shoulders. To compensate for such shortcomings, however, they have long, thick manes and tails, and a horseman's keen eye will discern the great depth of girth, good back and short, strong croup. The Camargue horse also possesses a generous amount of bone, and if the feet are on the large side they are nonetheless hard and ideally suited to the environment. The Camargue horse never needs shoeing.

This hardy horse lives and even thrives on the poorest of food, for it can expect nothing apart from what can be scavenged from the seemingly endless stretches of swampland. Its food, therefore, consists mainly of tough grass and reeds, saltwort and similar plants, coarse fare which is shared with the horse's massive compatriots, the fierce black bulls of the Camargue.

The Camargue horse seldom exceeds 15 hh and its greatest visual asset is its beautiful colour—a colour which poets

The foamy white coat of the Camargue horse gives it the name 'horse of the sea'

have likened to that of the sea foam. The silky white coat stands out in striking contrast to the jet black of the Camargue bull. The foal, of course, is not born white but is either iron grey, black or mottled brown, turning to white as it grows older.

The Camargue horse is as much a product of its environment as a Shetland or an Exmoor, and like them it is incredibly hardy. But it has its own particular characteristics. It does, of course, trot, but almost as if this style of movement were unnatural. More typical is a long, high-stepping walk and an exhilarating gallop, and these are the paces to which it has been trained for centuries.

Although some 40,000 acres of the Rhône delta have been salvaged for rice growing, the traditional occupation of the local cowherds or *gardians* is the raising of the black bulls for the bull ring. The Camargue horse is the vital link between man and bull, for without its efforts the bull industry could not survive. Apart from high courage, the white horse possesses an instinctive sure-footedness and an inherited ability to twist and turn as the *gardian* cuts out selected bulls from the herd.

From where did this horse come? As is the case with so many ancient breeds, nobody really knows. Thanks to the efforts of an enthusiast, Etienne Saurel, the Camargue horse is recognized as a specific French breed by the National Stud Services, but its origins, despite Monsieur Saurel's extensive research, remain much of a mystery. Possibly the horse is a descendant of the Asian or Mongol horses on which the Barbarians (Ostro-

The Camargue horse is extremely hardy, managing to live in the seemingly endless swampland on tough grass and reeds

goths and Vandals) invaded Europe, or it may even be a cousin of the Berber horse, to which it bears a certain resemblance. The most likely hypothesis, however, is that the Camargue horse is a native breed, closely connected to the horse of Solutré, although even this theory is subject to some reservations.

Solutré is a small village in the Charollais region of France where, in the nineteenth century, a large deposit of horse skeletons was discovered. These skeletons were dated as being approximately 50,000 years old. The interesting point in this connection is that these skeletons of European wild horses bore a remarkable resemblance to the modern horses of the Camargue. Clearly, there have been continual admixtures of blood since those early days, but on balance the conclusion must be that the Camargue horse is indeed indigenous to its particular area of France.

It is possible that Spanish horses were once present in this area and before them the horses of conquering Moorish invaders. Certainly in this part of France the ancient horse-lore of the Iberian Peninsula, traceable to the Moors, still survives in the person of the modern *gardian*—France's cowboy. He rides in a saddle that is unmistakably of Moorish origin and very similar to the Western saddle, high at the front and rear, and very heavy. The *gardian* wears schappes, too, but his stirrups, unlike those of the Western cowboy, are heavy cage-like affairs of iron, which have changed little since the Moors left Europe after their defeat at Poitiers by Charles Martel in AD 720.

The *gardian* rides in the fashion of the South American *gaucho* and the Californian cowboy, long-legged and holding the reins in one hand. In America to this day it is possible to watch systems of training, particularly in regard to bitting, that have not altered radically since they were introduced to the country by the sixteenth-century Conquistadors. But it is not necessary to go that far abroad, because such methods are still in evidence on the Camargue. Here the same transition has been made from a succession of nosebands (*bosal*) to a long-cheeked bit, the horse thereafter being ridden by the weight of the rein and the disposition of the rider's weight.

The *gardian* uses a lariat, too, but for the handling of the bulls he carries a long, forked pole (*pique*). For the rest, he relies upon the agility and guts of the Camargue horse between his thighs.

The Camargue is a region of many moods, and is fierce, stark, grand, sweet and sad by turns, but sometimes it erupts into gaiety and colour with the traditional folk festivals that do so much to attract visitors. The tourists who converge on Sainte Marie de la Mer, the principal town of the Camargue, can watch the *gardians,* dressed in their finery, play fierce games that have their roots deep in history. Not surprisingly, one of these games involves bulls as well. The *gardians* gallop the beasts through the streets in a tight bunch, while the crowd of onlookers do their best to separate the individual bulls from the herd.

At present there are some 30 *manades* in the region, comprising 45 stallions (*grignons*) and some 400 brood mares. Because of the Camargue horses, perhaps, the region can look forward to an era of renewed prosperity from tourism; and if pony-trekking is introduced, the famous horses of the sea will certainly play their part in that as well.

For of this savage race unbent
The ocean is the element.
Of old escaped from Neptune's car,
full sure
Still with white foam flecked are they,
And when the sea puffs black from grey,
And ships part cables, loudly neigh
The stallions of Camargue, all joyful
in the roar;

George Meredith

The Andalusian horse

THE adulation accorded to the Arabian horse as the fountain-head of the world's breeds is in most respects justified, but there is no doubt that it has overshadowed the contribution made by the lesser-known Andalusian. In fact, the Andalusian was the acknowledged mount of captains and kings centuries before the Arabian became so popular, and the influence of its blood in Britain, Europe and the Americas, before the eighteenth century, was as great.

The origin of this noble horse is as obscure as that of most of the ancient breeds. In Spain it is held that the Andalusian is a native of that country owing nothing to any breed outside the Iberian Peninsula. A more probable theory is that the Andalusian was evolved when the Barb horses of the Moorish invaders were crossed with the light, agile horses native to Spain. It is also postulated that these Spanish horses were themselves descended from horses of Barb type that had wandered across from north-west Africa centuries before, when the Iberian Peninsula was still joined to Africa by a strip of swamp land.

A theory that does not hold much water, although it is frequently put forward by hippologists, credits the all-embracing Arab with prime responsibility for the Andalusian. There is, however, no historical evidence whatsoever to suppose that this was, in fact, the case, nor does the Andalusian show any of the pronounced characteristics of the Arab which are stamped indelibly upon breeds that have benefited from Arab blood.

Be that as it may, there is no doubt at all that, from the time of the Roman emperors up to the eighteenth century, the Andalusian was the first horse of Europe. Every crowned or coroneted head of state who had his portrait painted between the fourteenth and eighteenth centuries is depicted sitting proudly on a curvetting Andalusian. William Cavendish, Duke of Newcastle, the one acknowledged English master of *haute école*, called the Andalusian '. . . the noblest horse in the world, the most beautiful that can be. . . . fittest of all for a King in the day of Triumph.'

In Europe, the Lipizzaners of the Spanish Riding School of Vienna are direct descendants of the Spanish horse, the Andalusian. Nine stallions and twenty-four mares were brought to Lipizza in 1850 by the Freiherr von Khevenhiller, emissary of the Archduke Charles of Austria. The Frederiksborg, the Neapolitan and the Kladruber breeds used later in Lipizzaner breeding were also of Spanish descent. And very recently the Spanish School acquired another Andalusian from the Terry stud at Jerez de la Frontera, a young horse called Honroso VI.

It was the Andalusian that was the mount of the sixteenth century *conquistadores*, those intrepid adventurers who conquered a great part of North and South America for the Spanish crown. The blood of the Andalusian, introduced by the *conquistadores*, lives on in the American horses of today. It can be seen in the Quarter Horse, the Appaloosa, the Saddle Horse, the Palomino and others. Also of Andalusian descent are the Peruvian Paso, the Argentine Criollo and the Paso Fino of Puerto Rico. The Andalusian has also had an influence upon British breeds, notably the Cleveland Bay, the Hackney, the Connemara and the Welsh Cob.

In Spain today the Andalusian is still bred in its native region of Andalusia, in the south of the Iberian Peninsula. This is an area whose climate and pastures are remarkably like those of parts of Arabia. Jerez de la Frontera, where the Terrys, of sherry fame, maintain a notable stud, Seville and Cordoba are the principal centres. Altogether there are some 1,500 pure-bred Andalusians in Spain and they remain, as they have always been, a strictly luxury article. They are ridden as parade horses in the *ferias*. Wealthy owners give private exhibitions of *haute école*, much as did the Renaissance nobles on the same breed of horse, bringing to life the paintings of Velasquez and Van Dyke. The Andalusian is also the highly schooled mount of the gentleman bull-fighters, the *rejoneadores*.

The Andalusian is essentially the 'school' horse, just as it was during the Renaissance. It has enormous presence, displays noble proportions and is possessed of great agility and fire while being of a friendly, docile temperament. Most Andalusians are about 15.2 hh and are either white, grey, bay or a characteristic 'mulberry' colour. The head, sometimes with a hawk-like profile, is majestic and the neck is strong and in stallions well crested. The back is short and linked to broad quarters which give the Andalusian its agility and ability to perform the collected movements of the High School. The tail is set on rather low and both tail and mane are luxuriant and worn long. In action the Andalusian is spectacular. The breed is naturally high-stepping and extravagant, so much so that the Andalusian frequently 'dishes' in front, a feature much beloved by the Spanish *caballero*, although it would be frowned on in British horse circles. (When a horse dishes, its forefeet are flung out to the side as it moves.) It was the great parade horse of the Middle Ages.

The noble Andalusian is a worthy rival to the Arabian horse, which has at times overshadowed this beautiful breed

The Andalusian is still bred in its native region of Andalusia, where the Terrys, who produce sherry, have a noteworthy stud

In fact, the Andalusian would not be placed in a British show class, but then, beauty is in the eye of the beholder. The beauty of the Andalusian, as it moves forward so majestically with its high knee action, is different from that of British horses, but it is just as lovely to see. It is truly a quality riding horse.

No discussion of the Andalusian would be complete without mention being made of the devotion to the breed of the Carthusian monks of Jerez de la Frontera, who in the late fifteenth century laboured to keep pure the classic Andalusian horse at a time when breeding in Spain was largely influenced by the Neapolitan, and other horses of Central Europe. The monks owned hundreds of mares, all branded with their church bell symbol, and for the old horses they kept a special ranch where they could end their days in peace. No mare was ever sold. It was called Salto al Cielo, the 'Springboard to Heaven'.

The horses bred at the Jerez stud were known as Andalusian Carthusians and are still bred in Spain today. A few were successfully hidden from Napoleon's army during the Peninsula War. The majority of the remaining Andalusians are descendants of the horses bred at the Zapata stud, and are consequently known as Zapateros. The Zapatero herd was successfully hidden from the French armies and after the cessation of hostilities, the surplus animals were sold to Andalusian breeders who had lost their stock. The Zapata breed was originally chestnut or black, but two grey stallions were introduced about 50 years ago, and the breed has since become predominantly grey. Zapateros have won many awards at leading shows on the Continent and are part of the Military Stud at Cordova.

The Lipizzaner

THE Lipizzaner horse is a breed deriving its name from the tiny village of Lipizza near Trieste, formerly a part of the Austrian Hapsburg empire. This was the site, in the sixteenth century, of the court stud of Archduke Charles of Styria. The breed is, however, so closely connected with Vienna's Spanish Riding School that it would be impossible to consider the one without the other.

The first reference to the School dates from 1572 when a wooden arena was being constructed next to the Imperial Palace of the Hapsburgs in Vienna. Mention is made of a 'Spanish Riding Hall', but it was not, in fact, until 1580 that the Archduke Charles, the youngest son of the Emperor Ferdinand I and ruler of Inner Austria, Styria, Carinthia, Gorizia and Friuli, imported nine stallions and twenty-four mares from the Iberian Peninsula, at that time a part of the empire of the Spanish Hapsburgs.

These Spanish horses were settled at Lipizza in the Karst country, a harsh, limestone wilderness to the north and east of the upper end of the Adriatic, in what is today a region of north-western Yugoslavia. It took many years of skilful management to turn the inhospitable Karst into land capable of responding to cultivation and irrigation, but even at its worst it was an area ideally suited to encourage supreme hardiness in the stock reared upon it, together with good bone and feet of particular excellence. Indeed, this area of sparse vegetation, dominated by stony outcrops, had been a famous breeding ground for horses throughout the centuries. The Romans had reared horses around Aquileia, and after them the Venetians had bred the Karst horses, used in knightly tournaments and jousts, on the lands bordering the Timavus River.

These first Spanish horses, from whom the School takes its name, were the foundation stock of the Lipizzaner breed. Their descendants can be seen today performing the intricate patterns of the School Quadrille, or launching themselves high above the ground in the spectacular School leaps, in Vienna's Winter Riding Hall, Fischer von Erlach's baroque masterpiece. Completed in 1735, during the reign of Emperor Charles VI, the Hall has been the showplace of the School (with the exception of the war years) up to the present time.

Spanish horses or Andalusians, as we know them, were the supreme riding horses of the day, their price confining them to the stables of kings and great nobles. Indeed, the Andalusian had occupied this position, virtually unchallenged, for a very long time, and was to remain the most famous horse in Europe until the emergence of the Thoroughbred in the eighteenth century. No other breed could compare to the Andalusian as a 'parade' horse or for the highly collected *manège* riding which was the fashion of the period. 'It is the noblest horse in the world . . . and fittest of all for a King in the day of Triumph', wrote William Cavendish, Duke of Newcastle (1592–1676), one of the very few acknowledged British masters of the *haute école*. Certainly, for the Duke's purpose, for that of his contemporaries and for the Renaissance nobility of Europe, the Andalusian deserved such glowing praise. No horse could have proved itself more suitable, both physically and in temperament, for the stern disciplines of the *manège* than the Andalusian. It is, therefore, not surprising that Freiherr von Khevenhiller, the emissary of the Archduke Charles, should have turned to the Andalusians to be the founders of his master's court stud—indeed, there was little other choice open to him.

The exact origin of the Andalusian cannot be traced with any degree of certainty. Lady Wentworth, for instance, an expert with the knack of endowing the most facile generalization with an aura of authority, declared that the Andalusian 'appears to be descended from prehistoric stock'. This formidable lady had said much the same of other breeds, and since the truth of her assertion applies to all living things it does nothing whatsoever to expand our knowledge. What is most likely is that the Andalusian evolved during the course of the long Moorish occupation of Spain, when the Barb horses of the invaders were crossed with local horses and ponies such as the Sorraia and Garrano. From later crossings with Arabian stock sprang the horse we know today, a breed which combined all the best qualities of Oriental and native Spanish blood. By the end of the fifteenth century, the breeding of the Andalusian had become concentrated in three studs established by the Carthusian monks of Seville, Jerez and Cazallo.

The Andalusian influenced and contributed to the establishment of many famous breeds, among them the Friesian, the Kladruber, the Frederiksborg, the Anglo-Norman, the Neapolitan and, of course, the Lipizzaner. Until the seventeenth century, Andalusians were still being brought regularly to Lipizza from studs in Granada and Seville. However, in due course, outcrosses had to be introduced as the supply of suitable horses from Spain became increasingly limited. These were made from blood strains close to the Andalusian and, significantly, from one Arab, the grey Siglavy, born in 1810.

Lipizzaners at the stud farm in Piber, Austria. They are generally small horses, many not exceeding 15.2 h.h. However, they are strongly built and many live until they are thirty years old

The six principal sires to which all the modern Lipizzaners bred at Piber (the present-day stud for the Spanish Riding School) can be traced are: Pluto, born 1765 and bought from the Royal Danish Court Stud at Frederiksborg—a horse, like others from Frederiksborg, of Spanish descent; Conversano, born 1767, a black Neapolitan; Favory, born 1779, a dun Kladruber (also based on Spanish blood) from Bohemia; Neapolitano, a bay born in 1790, and brought in from Polesina in Italy; Siglavy, a white Arab born in 1810; and Maestoso, a white horse born in 1819. This last-named sire carried both Neapolitan and Spanish blood. Of the original female lines, fourteen still exist today.

In the past, frequent attempts were made to introduce English Thoroughbred blood but all ended in failure. On the other hand, the introduction of pure Arab blood proved very successful. Siglavy, the Arabian founding father of the breed, made a notable contribution to the distinctive white colouring of the Lipizzaner, and the Arabian influence in the modern inmates of the Spanish School is particularly noticeable, although, of course, the dominant features remain those of the Andalusian.

Deliberate attempts to breed for white were made from the time of the stud's establishment at Lipizza, as this colour was considered the most desirable for the official 'horses of the emperor'. However, in the early days of the breed, the colours were very varied indeed, and ranged from black through bay, dun and cream to spots, the last type being highly esteemed until well into the eighteenth century.

While on the subject of colour, it is worth drawing attention to the painting by the English artist George Hamilton of brood mares grazing at Lipizza. This picture, painted in 1727, shows a remarkable range of colour, including spots, as well as giving an excellent indication of the characteristically rocky landscape. The numerous engravings of Johann Elias Ridinger in the same period are similarly revealing and also portray in detail the classical movements involved in the work of the *manège*.

Today, most Lipizzaners are white, although in accordance with genetic laws, bays tend to appear from time to time. These horses, however, are not used for breeding, although one is usually kept at the School. Lipizzaner foals are born black, grey or brown, but gradually turn to pure white by the time they reach the age of seven to ten years.

For 350 years the stud at Lipizza supplied the needs of the Spanish Riding School, adhering strictly to a breeding policy based on selection by performance, a policy that has remained unchanged to the present day. However, during the course of World War One, the horses were at first transferred for safety to Laxenburg and also to Kladrub. Then, following the collapse of the Austro-Hungarian empire in 1918, the Austrian share of the Lipizzaners was moved to the old Austrian National Stud at Piber, near Graz in Upper Styria.

World War Two was to prove an even more traumatic experience for the School and the white horses. Between 1941 and 1942 the Piber Lipizzaners, as well as those from the state studs of Hungary, Czechoslovakia, Rumania and Yugoslavia (and unconnected with the School), together with the horses retained by the Italians after 1918 at Lipizza, were moved to the remount centre at Hostau in the Bohemian Forest. For a short period there was, therefore, an opportunity for the mixing of the various strains coming from these studs.

As the war approached its close, the German officials, rather than let the Lipizzaners fall into the hands of the Russians, did everything possible to ensure that their charges would come under the authority of the advancing Americans. On the orders of the American General Patton, United States forces, under Colonel Charles Reed, brought the horses from Hostau to the West on 28 April, 1945. Thus were the Lipizzaners, and with them the Spanish Riding School, saved for posterity.

The Lipizzaner is, in general, a small horse—many not exceeding 15.2 hh—but it is strongly built and endowed with the most equable of temperaments. The body, set off by a short, powerful neck, presents a picture of strength, with rounded quarters, heavy shoulders and short, strong legs. As a breed the Lipizzaner is slow to mature—a phenomenon frequently observed among established breeds reared on lands similar to the Karst. However, such horses have the advantage of a remarkable longevity, and the Lipizzaner is no exception. Stallions, the only horses used in the Spanish School, are frequently able to perform the demanding exercises when well over 20 years of age, and many live until they are 30 years old.

To what extent the Lipizzaner breed owes its 400 years of existence to the Spanish Riding School is difficult to say—clearly it must be almost entirely so as far as the Lipizzaners of Piber are concerned, but not nearly so much in the case of those at the remaining European studs. In

A Lipizzaner stud farm at Lipizza in Slovenia. All the foals are born black, turning white as they mature. Right: Princess Anne, on a visit to Vienna, puts a horse from the Spanish Riding School through its paces

those countries the Lipizzaner, although ridden, is primarily a carriage horse, and often a farm worker too. What, however, is beyond doubt is that without the Lipizzaner it is unlikely that there would still exist in the late twentieth century a Spanish Riding School dedicated to conserving the proud traditions of eighteenth-century classical equitation, based on the precepts and the manner of the greatest of the French masters, Pierre Robichon de la Gueriniѐre.

For many horse lovers the Lipizzaner has a special attraction. The beauty of its movements, its apparent delight in its work when ridden by an expert, the great tradition of horsemanship that is embodied in the Spanish Riding School, all these factors combine to create a mystique that is not easy to describe but is nevertheless very real. Many of us must have envied Princess Anne who had the opportunity—and the skill—to ride a Lipizzaner when she visited Austria with her parents on a State visit in 1969. Such a privilege is, of course, reserved for eminent riders who have displayed outstanding ability in the dressage ring.

It is a fact that no breed, except perhaps the Arab, gives rise to so much uncritical adulation as the Lipizzaner. Taking a more balanced and objective view, however, away from the romance of the bicorne-hatted riders, the glitter of the chandeliers in the Winter Riding Hall and the entrance of the dancing white horses to the music of Bizet, it is all too apparent that the eighteenth-century Lipizzaner has its limitations as a twentieth-century riding horse.

Only one Lipizzaner in recent years has competed in international dressage competitions and that one, Conversano Caprice, was privately owned. Broadly speaking, the lack of brilliance and particularly of extension in the Lipizzaner compares unfavourably with the immaculate elegance of the Thoroughbred or near-Thoroughbred. Similarly, the Lipizzaner is outclassed in other mounted sports by its lack of scope and speed. In fact, while the Lipizzaner performing under the lights may be a beautiful sight, there is not a shred of doubt but that it does not have the make and shape that would qualify it for inclusion in the first row of an average British show class.

Nevertheless, despite its shortcomings in mounted sports, the one thing for which the Lipizzaner has been selectively bred for 400 years it does supremely well—better, in fact, than any other horse in the world. By displaying the results of a logical training progression and for preserving something so intrinsically beautiful, the devoted riders of the Spanish School, over the centuries of its existence, deserve the gratitude of the world. And so do the horses that have made it all possible.

Horses of the Americas

SIXTY million years ago when man was no more than 'an unidentified lemuroid' there flourished on the earth a small animal no bigger than a fox, which had four toes on its front feet and three behind. In 1876 a relatively complete skeleton of this strange animal was discovered in the United States and was called Eohippus, the Dawn Horse, by the American scientists responsible for the discovery. From this skeleton they were able to prove that Eohippus was the ancestor of the modern horse and to show that, following stages of development spread over millions of years, the species *equus caballus*, genetically the horse as we know it, though much smaller and far removed in conformation from our twentieth century horse, evolved in North America about a million years ago and from there migrated over the then existing land bridges to Europe, Asia and the South American continent. North America can, therefore, claim with justification to have been the cradle of the horse.

For reasons which we shall never know, the horse finally became extinct in the American continents after the Ice Age and the consequent disappearance of the Bering land bridge. It did not return to the Western Hemisphere until the arrival of Christopher Columbus at the island of Hispaniola, now Haiti, in 1490. Columbus brought with him 30 horses and before his death, sixteen years later, the Spanish had begun the establishment of horse-breeding centres for Spanish America on the larger islands of the West Indies. After Columbus every expedition sailing from Spain for the New World took with it a complement of horses. It was not, however, until Hernan Cortes landed in Mexico in 1519 with 16 horses, 11 stallions, two of which were pintos, and five mares, that the horse was re-instated in the continent from which it had disappeared ten thousand years before. A hundred years later the horses had spread northwards and bred in sufficient numbers for the Indian tribes of the Western Plains to be mounted and European settlers on the east were importing horses from their own continent. Horses from England were brought to the Massachusetts Bay Colony in 1629 and some years before that date large numbers of Irish horses were exported to Virginia. As the influx of settlers accelerated and was extended to include colonists from more and more European countries so the number of imported horses increased and more variety was added to the American horse population by breeds coming from countries like Sweden, Finland and Holland.

Further impetus to American horse-breeding was given by the establishment of the first American racecourse at Long Island in 1666. The course, near to the site of the present Belmont Park, was laid out by Richard Nicolls who captured New Amsterdam, now New York, from the Dutch and became its first English governor. As Governor Nicolls intended, the sport of racing encouraged 'the bettering of the breed of horses' and although at that time the evolution of the English Thoroughbred was in its early stages there is little doubt that the pattern of the English racer was the one sought after by the colonists. By the end of the following century the Thoroughbred was being imported in significant numbers and was becoming a major influence in American breeding.

In terms of the world's history four hundred years is of little account but within that incredibly short space of time the conglomerate of races that had crossed the seas from the Old to the New World had been welded into a nation that has become the most powerful in the world.

In that same short period the continent which had seen the origin of *equus caballus* but for thousands of years had not supported a single equine developed a horse population of such variety and size as to be virtually unrivalled throughout the world. The Thoroughbred, which exists in larger numbers in North America than anywhere else in the world, derives directly from the early English imports and has been a major factor in the development of specific American breeds. Of equal importance in the American horse culture was the early presence of the Spanish horses, whose descendants formed the wild mustang herds of the

The Appaloosa (left) is an ancient breed and was developed by the Nez Perce Indians, but was not recognized until 1938. The standardbred (right) is an admixture of the Narragansett, the Morgan but principally the Thoroughbred

prairies. These horses and their descendants have acted as a foundation for many breeds and without doubt are responsible for the existence of the spectacular and colourful Palominos, pintos and so on, which are so much a part of the American heritage.

The original Spanish horses were from Andalusia in Southern Spain. The Andalusian horse, which up to the eighteenth century was the foremost in Europe, was the result of the long Moorish occupation of the eighth century when the Iberian Peninsula was inundated with the Barb horses of North Africa. These horses, bred with the indigenous Spanish horse, produced the Andalusian, possibly after a further cross with Arabian horses, although many Andalusian enthusiasts will deny the existence of Arab blood in the breed. Be that as it may, the Spanish horses were well equipped to survive and thrive in hot, dry climates on sparse food and were blessed with extraordinary qualities of soundness and endurance.

When the later imports from Northern Europe, including the all-important Thoroughbred, are added it is not surprising that from this wealth of equine potential a vigorous people, unfettered by the conventions of the Old World and occupying a vast land of contrasting climate and terrain demanding horses suited to every kind of purpose, should have created a horse population unique in its infinite variety.

The Morgan (below) is a good all-rounder and makes an excellent show horse, pleasure horse, harness horse, as well as being able to compete in weight-pulling

Some of the American breeds have, of course, virtually disappeared. The wild Spanish mustang which became the cowpony from which eventually the Quarter Horse was bred, is almost gone, a handful only being preserved by enthusiasts. The Narragansett Pacer, one of the earliest established American breeds, is itself extinct but its blood is found in the ancestors of the Standardbred and it was also a part ancestor of the Quarter Horse.

The Narragansett Pacer took its name from Narragansett Bay on Rhode Island where it was the favourite of the property owners having large farms in the area. When racing was re-established in Restoration England under Charles II, the popularity of the old ambling and pacing horses declined and many of the best found their way to North America, particularly to New England. These horses, often crossed with Spanish stock brought up from the south, founded the Narragansett Pacer. The popularity of the breed, particularly amongst the planters of the West Indies, was the cause of its ultimate demise. The planters, appreciating the easy pacing gait which made the constant supervision of the sugar-cane fields a less arduous task, bought these horses in such large numbers that eventually the supply dried up and the Narragansett as such ceased to exist.

None the less the Narragansett made a very large contribution to a tradition of harness racing in America, one that was lost in Britain when flat racing caused the British to spurn the old trotting and pacing breeds. Today, America has over 800 trotting tracks and the sport attracts as large a following as flat racing.

The modern trotting horse, and possibly the world's superlative performer between the traces, is the American Standardbred evolved from an admixture of breeds including the Narragansett and Morgan but dependent principally on the Thoroughbred Messenger (1780) which traced his descent from the Darley Arabian, the direct line being through Mambrino, his sire, to Engineer, Sampson, Blaze and Flying Childers, the first great racehorse. Mambrino was, in fact, backed to trot 14 miles in an hour to the tune of 1000 gns by his owner, Lord Grosvenor, a wager that was not taken up, whilst Blaze was also the sire of Old Shales, the foundation of the Norfolk Roadsters. It was one of Messenger's great-grandsons, however, Hambletonian (known as Rysdyk's Hambletonian), a

horse foaled in 1840, which gave the Standardbred its outstanding trotting and pacing ability through the 1335 offspring sired by him between 1851 and 1875. Some 90 per cent of all Standardbreds stem from this single horse.

The name Standardbred arises from the early practice of establishing a speed standard as a requirement for inclusion in the American Trotting Register (the Standardbred became an official breed in 1880) of 2 minutes 30 seconds over a mile for trotters and 2 minutes 25 seconds over the distance for pacers. The first sub two-minute mile was trotted by Louis Dillon (1 minute 58.5 seconds) in 1903 and in 1971 Steady Star paced a mile free-legged (without hobbles) in 1 minute 52 seconds, an average speed of 33.03 mph.

The Standardbred, in comparison to the Thoroughbred, is less refined in appearance. Generally, the breed is also longer-bodied, shorter-legged and more common in the head. There is, however, enormous power in the quarters and the action, in a good horse, is completely straight and true as it must be if the legs are not to suffer damage.

The most numerous of the American breeds and arguably the first developed on the continent is the Quarter Horse. Over 800,000 are registered in the USA and in 42 other countries and the Quarter Horse can therefore lay claim to being the world's most popular horse. Although the Quarter Horse, from which was developed the Canadian Cutting Horse, is regarded as the supreme cow-pony it did not originate in the West but in the east among the Colonial Seaboard Settlements of the Carolinas and Virginia. The English colonists, bringing with them their inherent love of racing, crossed the best of the Spanish mares with imported British stallions 'of the blood'–the Thoroughbred was not then invented–and also reversed the process, mating Spanish stallions to English mares. These horses performed every sort of work in harness and under saddle but their fame stems from their extraordinary speed over rough tracks hacked out of the wilderness or even over the length of the village street, both of which were short in distance, seldom being more than 440 yards, or a 'quarter' mile.

With the coming of the Thoroughbred and the introduction of oval tracks allowing long distance races, the Quarter Horse went into a temporary eclipse and moved with the white man to the West where he quickly developed the inherent 'cow-sense' which made, and still makes, him the indispensible partner of cattlemen everywhere. Today he is the all-round pleasure horse and the star of the rodeo contests, which are America's second largest group of equestrian spectator sports and bid to rival the popularity of baseball. Nor is the Quarter Horse neglected in respect of his racing ability. Short-distance racing has experienced a revival and the Quarter Horse competes for one of the world's richest prizes, the All American Futurity Stakes worth around $600,000.

The Tennessee Walking horse, which is no longer seen in Europe, is considered to be the most comfortable ride in the world. It literally glides along the ground

The Quarter Horse, standing around 15 h.h., is compact, chunky and possessed of extraordinary massive and muscular quarters. His breed society, the American Quarter Horse Association, was founded in 1941 at Fort Worth and employs over 200 people to operate the world's largest equine registry.

Equally well known, if less numerous, is the Morgan Horse but unlike the Quarter Horse its descent is from one foundation sire of exceptional strength and merit, whose name was originally Figure but who is better known by the name of his second owner, Justin Morgan, who took him as a two-year-old in payment of a bad debt around the year 1795. He was supposed to have been foaled in West Springfield, Massachusetts and he

certainly lived his life after passing into Morgan's hands (and many others thereafter) at Randolph, Vermont. His breeding is at best obscure. Some authorities attribute the horse to a Thoroughbred named True Briton, and there was indeed a racer of that name who could conceivably have sired the colt. Those putting forward this theory often claim that the dam was a Wildair mare, that stallion being in the same ownership as True Briton but there is no conclusive evidence available in either case. A more likely theory, taking into account the appearance of the Morgan, particularly of the early ones and the statue of Justin Morgan himself at the University of Vermont Morgan Horse Farm which depict a less refined animal than the modern representatives of the breed, is that the horse was essentially a Welsh Cob with some Thoroughbred or Arab blood. This view is supported by the background of Morgan and his friends who from their names, like Evans and Rice (Rhys), must have been of Welsh extraction. Somewhat less tenuously, the name True Briton, even in those days, was firmly established amongst Welsh Cobs, many of which went to America.

Whatever the truth Justin Morgan was one of the world's remarkable horses. His life was one of unremitting labour. He worked all day at the plough, clearing woodland, dragging heavy loads and was forever being matched in weight-pulling contests so severe that it was nothing short of a miracle that a horse of his size, about 14 h.h. and weighing around 800 lb, could attempt such feats let alone beat all-comers. In addition he was raced under saddle and in harness, never being beaten, as well as performing his numerous stud duties. As a sire he was of unprecedented prepotency, transmitting his qualities to his descendants.

Today's Morgan is just such an all-rounder, a show horse and a pleasure horse, a harness horse and still able to compete in old-fashioned weight-pulling. He may be more refined than his illustrious forebear but in essentials he is a replica of that exceptional horse.

America's supreme show horse is the Kentucky Saddler, or to give him his modern name the American Saddlebred. Although the show ring is his *métier*, the Saddlebred was developed as a pure utility horse by Kentucky planters who spent

The Tennessee Walking horse (top) has a foundation stock which includes blood from the following; the Narragansett and Canadian Pacers, the Arab and the Thoroughbred. The Saddlebred (left) is Americas Supreme Show horse. The Quarter Horse (right) is the most numerous American breed

America nurtures more 'colour' breeds than any other country and the Palomino (left) is both very numerous as well as highly prized. Chincoteague ponies (above) are native to the island of chincoteague which is off the coast of Virginia

long days in the saddle and appreciated both comfort and an aesthetic appearance. Saddlebreds, as far as the show ring is concerned, come in three types: the harness horse, which performs at the walk and the animated park trot; the Three-Gaited Saddler, shown with 'roached' (hogged) mane and tail, which performs at walk, trot and canter and the outstandingly spectacular Five-Gaited Saddler. This horse in addition to the three basic paces is shown at the slow-gait, an elevated distinct four-beat pace in which each foot is poised momentarily before touching the ground, and at the 'rack'. This latter is the slow-gait at full speed that can cover a mile in as little as 2 minutes 19 seconds.

Although a number of breeds have contributed to the production of the Saddlebred, amongst them the Morgan, the early Narragansett and the Canadian Pacer (a horse originating in France and having an ambling gait), the foundation sire was the Thoroughbred Denmark (1839) and his son Denmark 61 out of a pacing mare.

The Saddlebred with his high, vertical and extravagant action and his rounded, compact body, in no way, however, resembles the Thoroughbred; rather he looks for all the world like a Hackney, which is not surprising when one considers his breeding.

Another American horse, continuing the easy-gaited tradition now lost in Europe, is the Tennessee Walker, claimed to be the most comfortable ride in the world and the most 'confidential'. The horse literally glides along in a four-beat pace that is half walk, half run and entirely relaxing. The foundation stock of the Walker, once known as the 'Turn-Row' for his ability to inspect crops row by row without damaging the plants, is a real mixture of bloods: Canadian and Narragansett Pacers spiced with Arab, Thoroughbred, Morgan and Standardbred. The Walking Horse Breeders Association, founded in 1935, designates a Standardbred as the foundation sire. This was Black Allan, who was useless on the track because of his fixed ambition to race at the walking pace.

To complete the trio is the Missouri Fox Trotter, an old but lesser known breed originating in Missouri's Ozark Hills in around 1820. Bred from Thoroughbred, Arab and Morgan stock the Fox Trotter has in more recent years benefited from Saddle and Walking horse blood but still retains his typical broken gait, fore feet walking, hind feet trotting.

The American Indian, specifically the Nez Perce tribe living in and around the Palouse Valley of Idaho, is largely responsible for the colourful, spotted Appaloosa. The breed is very ancient and horses of similar markings can be seen in early Chinese and Persian art forms. Their ancestors possibly came to Spain from Central Asia and reached the Nez Perce by way of Mexico. Appaloosa is a corruption of Palouse or Palousy. The breed suffered a decline in the years between the wars but its striking appearance, hardiness, speed and tractability resulted in a renewed popularity. It was not, however, recognized as an official breed until 1938.

In general, America relies for its ponies on importations from the British Isles, but it has one recognized, all-American pony which, although by European standards would not be considered long enough established to be accorded 'breed' status, is none the less indisputably defined. It is called the Pony of the Americas and it is remarkable for the reason that it exists entirely through the efforts of one man, Leslie Boomhower of Mason City, Iowa. In 1956 Mr Boomhower crossed a Shetland stallion with an Appaloosa mare and created a miniature of the famous spotted breed. Ponies to be registered in the Stud Book must fulfil stringent specifications, which include the characteristic markings of the Appaloosa and be between 11.2 h.h. and 13 h.h. In the short space of time which has elapsed since Mr Boomhower began his experiment to produce an American pony over 13,000 registrations have been made with the Pony of the Americas Club.

It should not be thought, however, that America has no 'native' pony stock. 'Wild ponies are still to be found on the islands of Chincoteague and Assateague, off the coast of Virginia and Maryland. Probably these ponies are descended from animals abandoned in the early colonial days and, although annual sales are held following Pony Penning Day in July, when the ponies swim the channel dividing the two islands, little if any effort has been made towards improvement. In general these animals are stunted horses without pony quality and lacking in defined type.

America, itself a colourful, vital land, also nurtures more 'colour breeds' than anywhere else. Palominos are numerous and much prized, as are the pintos and paints that were so highly esteemed by the cow-punchers and even the Albino, although suspect to the experienced horseman, is bred selectively.

Despite its own inherited equine wealth America maintains large numbers of imported breeds. There is a large Arab population, there are heavy horses of all kinds, German Hanoverians, Trakehners, Holsteins, Cleveland Bays and every sort of British native pony, most of which have their own American breed societies.

The trotting horse

TROTTING races have been held since time immemorial, but one of the oldest breeds whose records can be traced is the Orlov trotter. This breed dates back to 1777 when Count Alexei Grigorivich Orlov (1737–1808) started to breed them at the Khrenov stud. He put a grey stallion called Polkan, a descendant of a pure white Arab called Smetanka, to a dun Dutch mare and bred the famous grey stallion Bars I. This horse, foaled in 1784, was mated to mares bred the same way (Arabian-Dutch crossbreds) and he was so outstanding that his daughters were put back to him to set the type. It is a type that is still to be found, combining elegance with superlative action, especially at the trot.

The Orlov breed was already well dispersed at the beginning of the nineteenth century. It has always been subjected to systematic tests on racecourses, and races were first held in Moscow in 1799 on snow, the horses being harnessed to light sleighs. The Moscow Trotting Society was founded as long ago as 1834, well before the English Hackney Horse Society which was not founded until 1883, although trotting horses had been a feature of English life for some considerable time.

In 1836 the champion Orlov stallion, Bychok, covered 3·2 kilometres in 5 minutes 45 seconds. Thirty years later Poteshny had cut the time to 5 minutes 8 seconds. By 1894 the record had been reduced to 4 minutes 46 seconds, and the present record is 4 minutes 20·3 seconds.

As the breed had aristocratic connections, it was nearly destroyed during the Russian Revolution, but it was put under state control and is now bred in more than 35 state studs and in countless private establishments. Breeders have made extensive use of it in the development of the Don, the European trotter, the Torgel (an Estonian horse), the Voronezh and of course, the Orlov-Rostopchin, this last being a magnificent riding horse obtained very largely through in-breeding at the end of the nineteenth century. It has also improved the American Standardbred.

Outstandingly well proportioned, and almost entirely free from unsoundness of bone, the Orlov trotter is a horse of genuine quality. As well as being engaged in trotting races, both in sulkies and sleighs, it is equally suited to dray and farm work. The Oriental head is supported by a long, arched neck set on medium withers and oblique, muscular shoulders. The croup is comparatively long and broad, and the legs and tendons are solid and strong. The most common colours are grey, black and bay, and chestnuts are very rare. The Orlov Stud Book has fixed the maximum height at 16.2 hh for stallions and 15.3 hh for mares.

The Russian trotter was evolved by crossing Orlovs and American trotters about 80 years ago. The latter started to beat the Orlovs on the racecourse in the nineteenth century, and so Orlov mares were put to American stallions, especially to the record holder of that time, Cresceus. Though 156 American stallions were used, only six produced offspring which can still be traced back in the records of the Russian trotter. Though faster than the Orlovs, the cross-breds were smaller and lacked the outstanding conformation which made the Orlov so suitable for improving the agricultural horses. By 1940 a programme of selective breeding, which concentrated on size and conformation as well as speed, had been completed, and today the Russian trotter is almost as big as the Orlov. The record speed for 3.2 kilometres is 4 minutes 10.4 seconds.

The American trotters developed from the imported English pacers and amblers which were sold abroad when Charles II established racing at Newmarket. The British public then lost interest in trotting races–an interest it never regained, although trotting and races for trotters is an international sport. The Standardbred evolved from pacers (whose trot is lateral, rather than diagonal) and Norfolk trotters. It has achieved the status of a Thoroughbred in trotting and pacing circles. Both trotters and pacers are included in the Standardbred Stud Book.

Until 150 years ago, pacers and trotters were raced together. Today they run separately, but there are champions capable of great feats in both, the fastest of these being the so-called 'doublegaited' horse, Steamin' Demon, with a record of 1 minute 59·2 seconds in the trot and 1 minute 58·8 seconds in the pace, totalling two miles in 3 minutes 58 seconds.

All but ten per cent of modern American trotters can be traced back to a stallion called Rydsyck's Hambletonian, which was a son of Hambletonian X, a sire which first appeared in 1849 and can be traced back to the imported Thoroughbred stallion, Messenger, through his sire and dam.

The height of the breeders' ambition was always to produce a horse that was

Right: trotting races. These races have an ancient history. Today this sport is popular in America and on the Continent

8

capable of trotting the mile in two minutes, or a kilometre in 1 minute 14·6 seconds. The first to do so was a filly, Lou Dillon, in 1903.

The Standardbred is a horse of excellent temperament, willing and full of courage. It is also suited to draught work. It has a medium-sized head, a profile that is mainly straight, lively eyes, long ears, long sloping shoulders with plenty of muscle, a long humerus and short cannon bones. The withers are often ill-defined and the back long, with a somewhat defective transition to the hindquarters. The rump is high and sloping, the quarters strong and muscular. The hind legs are long with cow hocks, long pasterns, and well-made feet that are on the large side. Bay is a common colour but chestnuts, blacks, and, more rarely, greys and roans are also found. Height varies from 15 to 16.2 hh.

The Americans had been breeding trotters on English lines for more than a century when the Norman coach-horse breeders decided to do the same in France in 1835, eventually producing the Anglo-Norman trotter. As foundation stock they chose their own local breed, already refined by Arab and German blood brought back by Napoleon's victorious armies. They then went to England for their stallions, but instead of buying Thoroughbreds they selected the English hunter-type, one of which, the half-bred Young Rattler, figures in the pedigree of every modern French trotter.

These stallions improved the heavy Norman mares and eventually Thoroughbred blood was introduced, the two most notable examples of which were The Heir of Linne and Sir Quid Pigtail. Elegance, now the only missing link, was introduced by the use of Norfolk trotters, which the French trotters still resemble. Finally, American and Orlov stallions were used. Until 1940 the Stud Book was open to Anglo-Norman horses able to race over a kilometre in public in 1 minute 42 seconds. In 1941 it was closed to all but the progeny of a previously registered sire and dam, and from January 1, 1971, the offspring of brood mares were excluded until they reached the age of six.

Since trotting races started in France, in 1836, the breed has steadily increased in numbers, and there are at present an estimated 6,000 in France alone. Among them is the fastest trotter in Europe, Jamin, which holds the record for the mile of 1 minute 59·6 seconds, set up in 1960. Although the horse is a notoriously late maturer, those with potential are given their initiation to the racecourse in the special events for two-year-olds, which were instituted in 1950. The horse may run either in harness or under saddle.

A horse of magnificent temperament, the Anglo-Norman trotter is a powerful athlete, not yet fixed to a standard pattern, but one whose disproportions between the forehand and the hindquarters are curiously suited to the vigorous mechanics of the racing trot. Its most distinctive points may be listed as follows: long and widely spaced ears, high withers, wide neck, low-set tail and strong, well-defined hocks. The legs are hard and fine, the feet on the large side and ideally suited for soft ground. The overall picture is that of a well-made horse combining power with elegance. The average height is 16 hh, and the horse has more substance than American trotters.

Mounted trotting races are still popular in France, but the driven trotters hold their own in Italy, Germany, Scandinavia and the USA. In the 1950s Jamin, from the famous Rouge-Terres stud, went to the USA and beat the best American horses on the heavily banked tracks of the Roosevelt Raceway.

The German trotter, longer-barrelled than the French, is of more recent origin. Not until 1874 was the first trotting club formed in Hamburg, and the first stud was founded 11 years later. The breed was originally based on the Orlov, but American and, later, French blood was to effect the greatest improvement.

There are now some 2,500 trotter mares in Germany–double the number of Thoroughbreds–and the most famous stallion was Epilog, whose dam was French-bred. This horse covered 1,000

Below: A trotting race about to take place. Trotters are bred for speed and a showy leg action

metres in 1 minute 18·6 seconds and his most distinguished son, Permit, holds the current record with 1 minute 17·3 seconds.

Although trotting matches were held in England before flat racing was developed, they were soon superseded by it, and the English trotter, or Hackney horse, was bred for action and conformation rather than for great speed.

Although the origin of the trotting horse in England, and in particular of the Hackney, is largely a matter for conjecture (in common with any other long-established breed), it is reasonably certain that it is descended from Thoroughbreds and from the heavier breeds.

It is a generally accepted theory that the Darley Arabian, one of the three founders of the General Stud Book of Thoroughbred horses, also left his mark on the modern Hackney as the sire of the chestnut Flying Childers. Foaled in 1715, out of Betty Leedes, Flying Childers was in his turn the sire of Blaze. The latter, which was foaled in 1733, afterwards travelled in Norfolk where the excellence of the Hackneys, which were known as Norfolk Trotters, was already well established. They had been bred earlier by the use of Eastern sires and trotting mares, as well as Flemish light draught mares.

Blaze was the sire of the first Shales, of which there were several. He was foaled in 1755. Ten years later came Driver, another son of Blaze. Driver was the sire of Jenkinson's Fireaway (1780) and West's Fireaway (1800), and from this line came the great Danegelt, born in 1879. He enjoyed a remarkable career, both in the show ring and at stud, during the course of his fifteen years. West's Fireaway was the sire of Burgess's Fireaway (1815), which was in turn the sire of Wildfire, another great name in the history of the Hackney. He was foaled in 1827, and eight years later his son Phenomenon was born–sire of Performer, grand-sire of Sir Charles, and great grand-sire of Denmark, the sire of Danegelt.

Phenomenon was sold to Yorkshire as a three-year-old, to be crossed with Yorkshire mares, and, standing for many years with Mr Robert Ramsdale at Market Weighton, improved the breed very considerably. In the course of time the Yorkshire Hackney was said to have become bigger and more powerful than its East Anglian counterpart.

Old Shales, the ancestor of many famous modern Hackney strains, had a trotting record of 17 miles an hour, which was a very useful speed on the bad roads of that time. Philomena, a twelve-year-old 14·2 hh mare, trotted four miles in less than eleven minutes in 1800. But these early Hackneys, or Roadsters, which had to do odd jobs about the farm and carry a burly farmer and possibly his wife to market, were probably much stockier than the show Hackney of today, which requires both elegance and high quality action.

Denmark and Lord Derby II were the most celebrated of the Yorkshire Hackney sires, while Confidence was the most famous sire in Norfolk. Denmark was a chestnut, foaled in 1862 and standing 15.2 hh. He was by Sir Charles out of Merryman, which won at the Great Yorkshire Show at the age of 23 with Denmark as a foal at foot. Denmark was destined to become an extremely fashionable sire, and Sir Walter Gilbey paid 5,000 guineas for his most famous son, Danegelt, while his daughter Ophelia was said to be the greatest brood mare in the history of the Hackney breed. Although Denmark won many prizes in the show ring, his achievements at stud were more distinguished.

Lord Derby II, a dark brown horse, was foaled in 1871, by Lord Derby out of Nancy, and his blood, especially when crossed with that of Denmark, has produced some of the most illustrious Hackneys. A third Yorkshire stallion, Triffett's Fireaway, was a noted sire of brood mares, in particular of Ophelia's dam, Jenny Bother'em. Most of the top English Hackneys now trace back to the brown stallion Mathias, born in 1895.

Above: a Hackney horse. Most of the top English Hackneys trace back to the brown stallion Mathias, born in 1895

In conformation, the good Hackney follows the general lines of any other horse. It must have good shoulders which are paramount for smoothness of action. Depth of girth is not so apparent as in the hunter, for the depth of the back ribs produces a comparatively level lower line. There must be an overall impression of activity, strength and symmetry, with great gaiety and elegance. The action is characteristic and very important, demanding dash, fire and freedom with smoothness and levelness. Immense liberty in the shoulder action is essential, while the hind legs provide propulsion, and crisp hock action is as important to the expert as brilliant action in front. The Hackney stands from 14.3 to 15.2 hh or higher and may be bay, brown, black or chestnut, often with white markings which increase its showiness in conjunction with its unique action. The present-day Hackney is very popular in Holland and North America as well as in England. Hackney ponies are now considered to be a separate breed and are the result of crossing Hackney stallions with pony mares.

Polo Ponies

THE breeding of polo ponies has altered more in recent years than has the breeding of any other horse or pony. The reason for this is the increase in the desired height of playing ponies. In former times the height limit was 14.2 hh. Then the limit was raised to 15 hh before it was abandoned altogether.

The first polo and riding pony show was held in London in 1900, some thirty years after the game, which is of very ancient origin, was brought to England by British Army officers who had discovered its delights while serving on the north-west frontier of India. At this first show, stallions and mares of the right type and size were approved for inclusion in the stud book of the National Pony Society and these became the forbears of the English polo pony. Most of them were of unknown pedigree, though some had Arab blood in them and others were related to the Hackney. In recent years, foreign blood–mainly from the Argentine–has been introduced in order to increase the pony's height. Entry to the stud book was then achieved by a veterinary inspection for soundness, while a council member of the Society inspected the animal for type. If all was in order, the animal was then accepted for registration as an approved stallion or mare.

It was no easy task to effect an increase in height while still retaining pony character, especially as some of the stallions were small Thoroughbreds, many of them winners under Pony Turf Club rules. One of the best-known and most successful breeders before the First World War was the late Sir Tresham Gilbey, who adhered most faithfully to the true polo-bred ponies, though he used the full-sized

Thoroughbred stallion Bridgwater for his small mares and also the Thoroughbred pony stallion, Wild Tint. After the war was over, several new breeders came to the fore, among them the late Herbert Bright who, like Sir Tresham, kept as far as possible to polo-bred stock. He made famous the 'Silverdale' prefix, and his polo-pony stallion Silverdale Loyalty was one of the most famous sires of all time.

Perhaps the most successful of modern breeders is Miss Marguerite de Beaumont, who established a dynasty on one remarkable foundation mare, the grey hack champion June XI, by the Thoroughbred Gars de Falaise out of a French Anglo-Arab mare called Betty. June had bred six foals to Thoroughbred horses during the war years before she became the unbeaten Champion Hack of 1946 for her owner, Mrs Noel Edwards, who was given her as a foal. She was produced under saddle by Count Robert Orssich, and when she was sold to Miss de Beaumont and retired to stud she had a further six sons and daughters, some by the late Henry Wynmalen's celebrated Hungarian-bred Arab, Basa Shagya. She bred many champions, and her daughters in their turn bred still more. In terms of show ring winners, June established a record which will stand unchallenged for a long time to come and the blood line she began is one of the most important.

Typical of the small Thoroughbred stallions, which have been used so successfully to breed polo ponies, were the late Lord Digby's Ack-Ack, Miss de Beaumont's Clieveden Boy (by Ujiji out of Fair Road by Fairway) and, perhaps best of them all, the late Miss Nina Jelley's Gay Presto. One of twins, which explains his lack of inches, he was sired by Precipitation out of a mare by Gainsborough. He died, aged 23, in 1968 but his son, Morning Magic, carries on the good work.

An exciting match at Windsor; stamina and speed are essential requirements in a polo pony, and both horse and rider must be well trained

HRH the Duke of Edinburgh in Jamaica, 1966. Royal participation in the sport has revived public interest in it

Gradually, with the decline in the number of polo players because of mechanization of the cavalry regiments, the outlet for these ponies began to be diverted from the polo field into the show ring. The small Thoroughbreds began to breed hacks instead, and though the polo pony blood is still available, it has been found more profitable to breed children's riding ponies.

When the sport of polo first spread across the world from India to the United States, the native ponies of each country were used – Chinese ponies in Hong Kong and Shanghai, Arabs in Egypt and the Sudan, and both Arabs and countrybreds in India. But soon the superiority of the better-bred Australian ponies, the Walers, became evident, and by the beginning of the First World War they had come to dominate the high-goal games in India, then the home of world polo.

Competitive international matches between the USA and England were at their height at the turn of the century. England won the Meadowbrook Cup for the last time in 1914, the riders being mounted on small Thoroughbreds. But when the height restriction was removed, size and pace were at a premium, though it was eventually agreed that the best height for polo ponies was between 15 hh and 15.2 hh. It was also agreed that the short-striding pony was the easiest to manoeuvre, rather than the long-striding Thoroughbred, and so the cow-pony began to appear in second-class transatlantic polo. These ponies were cheap to buy and to ship, and were ideal for teaching beginners the rudiments of the game, although they were common and lacking in speed.

The primary requirements of the polo pony are that it should have speed, stamina, courage, balance, and the right temperament – neither too excitable nor too lethargic – and from the beginning of the century, the Argentinians had been experimenting with the use of Thoroughbred blood on their native Creollo mares. With their enormous opportunities for cheap production, they succeeded in upgrading their stock to the extent that by 1930 they were producing a pony that looked like the English Thoroughbred, but which was tougher with better bone.

In the 1930s, there were more Argentine ponies playing in high-class polo in the USA than any other type. Because of World War Two, the sport was not played for six years, either in England or the USA, but it continued in the Argentine and a great many ponies continued to be bred on the best lines. Polo was started again in England and America in 1947, and by this time the Argentinian players dominated the scene, while their ponies were the major source of supply for international matches. They remain so today. They average 15.2 hands high, and only mares that have proved themselves in the game are used for breeding. They now comprise an individual breed which is exported all over the world wherever polo is played.

The polo pony requires all the good points of the first-class riding horse and indeed is, in effect, a Thoroughbred in miniature. The head should be well bred, the neck fairly long and convex, the shoulders well sloped and freely used, the back short, the loins and quarters strong and powerful, the body deep and well coupled. Knees and hocks must be close to the ground and the pasterns well sloped. The ability to twist and turn at speed, as well as general soundness, is absolutely essential.

The standard of training must be very high, for it has to go on two tracks when riding off another pony. This is the ability to move laterally, making two parallel tracks with the fore and hind legs respectively. It must be able to do a 'flying change' at the canter, that is, changing the leading leg without breaking down to a trot. A polo pony must be able to pull up from full gallop in a few strides and do the same exercise in reverse, and it must be able to do pirouettes. The polo pony must also move smoothly to facilitate the hitting of the ball, and it must be staunch enough to face oncoming ponies and riders. It must also do all its work when ridden with one hand on a loose rein.

Thus it must be very well trained in ordinary school work before it is ever introduced to the stick and ball. A few ponies remain ball-shy, but most of them accept it quite quickly. All work is done at the walk or the canter, for polo ponies never trot.

Polo ponies often tend to poke their noses forward and carry their heads high, and most of them need to be ridden in a standing martingale, which also doubles as a neck strap for the rider. Even so, their mouths take a good deal of unavoidable punishment, for the aids have to be applied swiftly and vigorously and the key to all polo tactics is the abrupt stop from full gallop and the turn of 180 degrees.

Above and left: two moments at a match in Cowdray Park in August 1970. The game was brought to England from India

Few good polo players, moreover, are really top-class horsemen, though there are the usual exceptions to prove the rule. The good ball-player who is a moderate horseman will always manage to get by on the polo ground, although, however good the horseman, if he has not an eye for a ball he will never be able to play polo.

The wear and tear on a polo pony's legs is considerable, and supporting bandages are a very necessary part of its equipment. Green ponies are schooled in slow chukkas, and it takes at least a season before a pony that has been well schooled along basic lines is ready to play in a tournament. Without the advantage of adequate basic schooling it will take a good deal longer than that.

In Britain, the fact that the Duke of Edinburgh and the Prince of Wales both play the game has undoubtedly increased public interest in a minority sport which would be well served by television, although England is no longer a top-class polo nation.

Working breeds of horse

Below: Shire horses ploughing. The tractor has largely replaced the horse in farming, but there are still a few farms in England that use Shire horses

IN the 1970s it may seem to many people that heavy draught horses are as much outdated as the knight in armour, their functions having been taken over by the machine. However, these horses continue not only to survive but to thrive, and there is no reason to think that they will not continue to do so. Each breed has its own Breed Society and Stud Book, and each holds an annual show with many entries. They are still used by farmers in some areas, and their use may increase as the world energy crisis becomes more acute. Brewers use them on short hauls in towns, for which purpose they are cheaper than motorized transport, and a better advertisement.

Heavy horses are found at most shows, and throughout the English-speaking world there are enthusiasts dedicated to the maintenance and improvement of the breeds which form a part of the national heritage. Additionally, quality British stock enjoys a fair export market. In Australia, New Zealand and in America the heavy horse is similarly popular.

Originally the heavy horse evolved as a work horse; later it became a weapon of war as the only mount capable of carrying the increasingly heavy armoured knight, the pride of the Middle Ages. In turn the knight became an anachronism but his horse lived on in agriculture and transport until, by selective breeding and development, a number of distinct breeds emerged.

By the late eighteenth century three definite and stabilized heavy breeds existed in Britain, although their origins go back far beyond that time. There was also a lighter 'working' horse of great antiquity, the Cleveland Bay, which had been known in the Cleveland district of North Yorkshire since medieval times. The three breeds were the Clydesdale, Shire and Suffolk Punch and, a hundred years later in the nineteenth century, they were to be joined by an imported heavy horse, the French Percheron.

Of these horses, the Clydesdale originated in Lanarkshire, in Scotland's Clyde valley, which was regarded as the best horse-breeding area of the country. The Clydesdale evolved as a result of using Flanders stallions on native mares and, by the time of the Industrial Revolution, it was becoming established as an active, quality draught horse, a good worker on the farm, and particularly well suited, because of the emphasis which the breeders placed on good feet, for haulage work in the urban streets. The Clydesdale Horse Society was started in 1877, and the Stud Book at about the same time.

The Clydesdale, not so massive as either the Shire or Suffolk, stands some 17 hh. The head is peculiar to the breed, being broad and flat-profiled. The Clydesdale gives an impression of being weak behind, because, one supposes, of the long quarters and a tendency towards 'cow hocks', but this is something which the breed is certainly not. White stripes on the face and pronounced white shanks are characteristics of the breed which carries heavy feather (hair) on the legs.

The Shire is a typically British product, almost as much as the bulldog, and is claimed to be the purest survival of the Great Horse. It is probably among the largest horses in the world, an enormously powerful, massive horse standing some 18 hh and weighing over a ton. The breed was founded on mares of the Old English Black horse breed and, as its name implies, its origin was in the 'shires' of England, particularly in the counties of Leicester, Derby and Stafford. The Shire may lack the longer stride of the Clydesdale but it steps high and is very active and capable of drawing great loads. A good Shire is able to pull 5 tons, and a pair, yoked tandem-fashion, has been known to move 18½ tons of granite.

The Suffolk Punch, the work horse of East Anglia, is a breed that can be dated back to 1506, although present-day

Above: two Shires at a ploughing match. These competitions are held at local County Shows, so that the ploughmen can show their skill

Suffolks are said to trace back to one great horse, Crisp's Horse of Offord, which was foaled in 1760. The Suffolk is always whole chestnut in colour, there being seven accepted shades ranging from bright to dark chestnut. The Suffolk stands about 16 hh, its great, well-ribbed body on short, clean, legs which have a very minimum of feather. Nonetheless, it weighs a ton or more, and is hard to beat as a worker. In addition to its strength, the breed is long-lived.

The Percheron, bred in the Perche district of France, was imported to England late in the last century. A breed society, the British Percheron Society, was formed in 1919. The area in England in which the horse is most popular is the Fen country of East Anglia, centred upon Cambridge. The Percheron is also extremely popular in the USA. Hundreds of Percherons were taken to America from France in the 1880s by a man named Mark Dunham. Grey and black are the only two permissible colours and the Percheron averages 17 hh. The breed's action is particularly free and active. The legs are short with tremendous bone, and have very little feathering. Its temperament is very docile. Altogether, the Percheron is an impressive example of a draught horse.

Finally, there is the native Cleveland Bay, not a 'heavy' horse by any means, but certainly in the past a considerable 'work' horse. The Cleveland Bay is also known as the Chapman horse. This name comes from medieval times when the breed was very popular among travelling salesmen, known as 'chapmen'. It filled a variety of roles superlatively well, being used as a pack-horse, on the farm, in harness and under saddle. Later it became a high-quality carriage horse and remains so today. It is also an exceptional hunter in its own right and crosses very successfully with Thoroughbreds to produce a lighter, faster horse that retains the characteristic hardiness and strength of bone. Half-bred Clevelands of this sort are used in harness and the Queen has a team that competes in the relatively new sport of three-day event driving. Clevelands are not numerous, but there is no reason to suppose that, with the constant demand for hunters and driving horses, they are in danger of extinction.

Bay is the only colour allowed and the breed is very sturdy and solid. The average height is 16 hh. The back must be not be too long, but strong and with muscular loins. The hindquarters should be powerful, level, with the tail springing well from them. The amount of bone should be 9 to $10\frac{1}{2}$ inches, measured below the knee. The Cleveland Bay Society was founded in the early 1880s and the first Stud Book was published in 1884.

The heavy horse breeds are extremely unlikely to disappear. Despite their huge size and enormous strength, the 'heavies' are extremely docile and easily managed.

Below: two Suffolk Punches. Nowadays these horses are mainly seen pulling brewers' carts round towns

Champion horses

WHAT makes a horse worthy of the accolade of 'Champion'? Its achievements count for a great deal, but the really great horses have a character about them that compels the public to take them to their hearts. Among these are horses like Arkle, Mill Reef, Golden Miller and Brigadier Gerard, all of which received in their day a great deal of public adulation.

But well before their time there was a racehorse which is entitled to be remembered as the champion of champions. Its name was Eclipse, and of it was said, 'Eclipse first, and the rest nowhere'. Eclipse was born in Windsor Great Park on April 1, 1764, the year of an eclipse of the sun, which gave the horse its name. Owned by the Duke of Cumberland, son of George II, its sire was a mediocre horse, Marske, and its dam Spiletta, which had run only one race in its life and was then soundly beaten. Yet the chance mating of these two was to produce a horse described as 'the most remarkable animal ever bred'.

Sold, on the Duke's death, to William Wildman for 75 guineas, Eclipse which, because of its uncertain temper, was virtually unmanageable, eventually ran its first trial at Epsom in 1769. An Irishman, Dennis O'Kelly, saw that trial and saw

Below left: Debbie West on Baccarat; right: Marion Mould on Stroller, the remarkable show jumping pony which won a silver medal at the Mexico Olympics. Far right: HRH Princess Anne on Goodwill

how easily Eclipse beat the opposition. In May of that year Eclipse ran its first race, a maiden for 50 guineas, to be run in two four-mile heats. O'Kelly placed bets all round on Eclipse, wagering that it would be 'Eclipse first, and the rest nowhere'. Eclipse won and O'Kelly made a fortune, sufficient to buy Eclipse for 1,750 guineas a year later. Under O'Kelly's careful management Eclipse ran 18 races and was never once beaten or even extended.

The significance of Eclipse in Thoroughbred breeding is not, however, confined to its racing performance. It raced when the ability to carry weight (12 stone and above) over long distances (four miles) at speed was the criterion of the turf. Eclipse went on to found a dynasty which is quite remarkable for its courage and staying power. Eclipse never won a Derby; it was 16 when the race was first inaugurated, but its descendants, among them Ormonde, Persimmon, Or, Stockwell, Hermit, Gladiateur and Galopin, are all famous Derby winners. Morston, winner of the 1973 Derby in two minutes 36 seconds, also traces its pedigree to Eclipse. In fact, of the 194 Derbys run, 144 (74 per cent) have been won by direct male descendants of Eclipse. Of the 15 winners of the Triple Crown, that is the 2,000 Guineas, the Derby and St Ledger (the supreme achievement of the racehorse), all but one are descended from Eclipse.

Another more recent racing star was Golden Miller, the wonder horse of the 1930s, which, until Red Rum won the Grand National in 1973, had held the course record for almost 39 years. Golden Miller's favourite course was Cheltenham and it won the Gold Cup in 1932, '33, '34, '35, and '36. Its greatest triumph was to win both the National and the Gold Cup in 1934, a feat never achieved before or since. During those five years, the Miller won another 14 out of 19 races and was acclaimed as the horse of the century.

The Miller was born in 1927 in an open shed in Ireland, the son of Gold Court out of Miller's Pride, neither of which had ever won a race. The stud fee paid for the mating was a mere £5. Furthermore, the Miller was a late developer and in its early days its trainer, Bristowe, did not think the horse would even make a passable hunter. However, once the Miller was in the ownership of the famous and eccentric Dorothy Paget there began a partnership which was to be unequalled in the annals of the turf.

Of more recent memory are Arkle, Mill Reef and Brigadier Gerard, the former a 'chaser and the other two flat racers. No horse within the last decade has inspired so much public affection as Arkle. It first showed that it was no ordinary horse in 1962 when it cruised past a goodish field of 27 runners to win a three-mile novice hurdle at Navan. But it was not until it won the Cheltenham Honeybourne 'Chase in the same year that its owner, Anne, Duchess of Westminster, its trainer, Tom Dreaper, and its jockey, Pat Taafe, began to see Arkle as a Gold Cup horse and a serious contender for the crown then held by Mill House.

Arkle first met Mill House in the Hennessy Gold Cup at Newbury in 1963. Arkle lost the race on that occasion, but next time, with another half dozen good races behind it, there was no repetition of the error. In one of the greatest Cheltenham Gold Cups ever run, Arkle beat Mill House convincingly. This was in 1964, Arkle's best season, and in October of that year it ran Mill House into the ground when winning the Hennessy at Newbury. Arkle won two more Gold Cups to complete the hat-trick. Then, in 1966, it ran its last race with a fractured pedal bone, in the King George VI 'Chase at Kempton. Skilled care repaired the injury but, wisely, Arkle's owner never raced the horse again, allowing her pet to spend its last days in retirement.

It was also an injury, and a far more serious one, that ended the racing career of Mill Reef. But in this case a remarkable feat of surgery repaired the broken leg sustained at exercise and allowed the horse to begin a new career as a Stud. Mill Reef is owned by the American enthusiast, Paul Mellon, and was bred at

Right: Mill Reef, whose brilliant career was ended by a broken leg. Below: Mill Reef's first foal and its mother

17

Above: Mary Gordon Watson on Cornishman V, the greatest event horse of its time. It was in the team at Munich

his Rokeby Farm in Virginia. By Never Bend out of Milan Mill, it arrived at Ian Balding's Kingsclere stables in 1969 and as a two-year-old won all four of the top two-year-old races, the Coventry Stakes, the Gimcrack, the Imperial and then the Dewhurst at Newmarket. In that season the horse won more prize money in England than any other horse of its age had ever done before.

As a three-year-old, Mill Reef went for the mile-long 2,000 Guineas and lost to the great Brigadier Gerard, undoubtedly the greatest miler of recent years. But it won the Derby in that year, 1971, over a longer course than the Guineas, as well as the Eclipse, the King George and Queen Elizabeth Stakes and the glittering prize of the French Prix de l'Arc de Triomphe, which it won in record time. In the following year Mill Reef had further triumphs, winning the Prix Ganay and the Coronation Cup. But the great race between it and the Brigadier in the Eclipse Stakes was never to take place. Mill Reef contracted rhinoneumanitis and had to be scratched and laid off. Then followed the incident of the broken leg which ensured that the horse would never run again.

Brigadier Gerard's career is as brilliant as that of Mill Reef, and is the result of carefully formulated breeding plans laid by its owners, John and Jean Hislop. The dam of the Brigadier was the mare La Paiva, whose dam, Brazen Molly, was a great-granddaughter of the legendary Pretty Polly. The Hislops chose as a sire Queen's Hussar, in whose pedigree the great Fairway featured prominently.

As a two-year-old, Brigadier Gerard won among others the top-class two-year-old race, the Middle Park Stakes, and as a result the Hislops were offered £250,000 for their horse. But it was not for sale. The Brigadier won 15 of its 16 races, including the 2,000 Guineas and the Eclipse Stakes, winning £203,213. In 1972, when it won the Eclipse, it also achieved the remarkable feat of winning the King George VI and Queen Elizabeth Stakes. The Brigadier, after its short and brilliant career, is one of the most highly valued horses in the world and has now begun a new career as a stallion at Newmarket's Egerton Stud.

Champions are not, however, confined solely to racing. They come in every equestrian sport. Whenever enthusiasts talk about show jumping, one name can never be overlooked. It is that of Foxhunter, the horse which became the 'grand seigneur' of world jumping.

Foxhunter was born in 1940. Its sire was a Thoroughbred and its dam was a hunter whose grand-dam had been a pure-bred Clydesdale. The horse seemed 'a natural' for jumping from the beginning, and in 1947 Foxhunter and its owner, Harry Llewellyn, began their famous partnership. At that time the British were still 'placing' horses at fences, and as a result were not in the running when it came to international jumping against the clock. It was largely through the example of Llewellyn and Foxhunter that British riders and horses were able to change their style and to learn the art of galloping round a course, which had to be mastered before they could expect international success. At home, Foxhunter was almost invincible and soon was beating the best of the Continentals on their own ground and making British teams a force to be reckoned with. Foxhunter represented Great Britain 35 times, had 71 international wins and is the only horse to have won the Royal International Horse Show's King George V Gold Cup three times. More important, however, is the fact that it was Foxhunter which helped to win Britain's first-ever Olympic Gold Medal for team show jumping in 1952.

If Foxhunter has become a legend, the same must be true of a very different sort of horse. In fact, Stroller was not a horse but a pony measuring no more than 14.1½ hh and for this reason its achievements are even more remarkable. Present-day show jumping courses at an international level are made up of big fences, some of them with formidable spreads, best suited to big, powerful horses of great range and scope. On some occasions the fences Stroller jumped were considerably higher than itself but, because of its extreme gymnastic ability, this pony was able to beat the cream of the world's jumpers.

Marion Coakes (now Marion Mould) and Stroller entered open jumping competitions in 1962 and three years later Marion became the Ladies World Champion, when she was only 18. She was also to be the youngest holder of the Queen Elizabeth II Cup, and a member of the British team which won the Nations' Cup on three occasions. But without doubt the peak of Stroller's career was reached at the Mexico Olympics, when it won a silver medal. Stroller was the first pony and probably the last to compete in the Olympics, let alone win a medal.

The sport of three-day eventing, the toughest and most demanding of all equestrian sports, has also produced notable horses: High and Mighty, Airs and Graces, Countryman, The Poacher and many others. Perhaps, indeed, an event horse should be considered the champion of all horses, since it has to excel in dressage, cross-country, and show jumping.

In 1959, a dark bay colt was born on a Cornish stud farm. Its dam was Polly Fourth, a well known point-to-pointer, and its sire was Golden Surprise, winner of 17 steeplechases and grandson of the great Hyperion. That colt was Cornishman V, destined to become the greatest event horse of its time. Bought by Brigadier Gordon-Watson, who wanted a top-class hunter, it was something of a handful at first, and threw its owner frequently. With perseverance and kindness, however, this horse became a superb hunter and, with its owner, won the Army Trophy in the Melton cross-country event. Then, in 1966, Cornishman started to event, ridden by the Brigadier's slightly built daughter, Mary. Two years later, Cornishman was to be in the British Gold Medal team at Mexico in 1968, although not ridden by Mary (who had a broken leg). Generously, the horse was lent to the team and ridden by Richard Meade.

In 1967 Mary was in the saddle again and at 18 she won the European Championship at Haras du Pin in Normandy. In the following year she and Cornishman won the World Championship at Punchestown, Ireland and in 1972 they were in the winning British team at Munich.

Yet another champion was a 14 hh chestnut pony mare. Its name was Pretty Polly, the show pony of all time, and matriarch of a line of riding ponies that has never been equalled. Pretty Polly was sired in Ireland by the Arabian Naseel out of a Thoroughbred-Welsh mare, Gypsy Gold. Its show-ring career started as a four-year-old in 1949 when it was the Dublin champion and then, bought by Mr Deptford, doyen of the pony rings, it began a career in England ridden by Davina Lee-Smith. Pretty Polly was virtually unbeatable, being a true child's pony with perfect movement, enormous presence and excellent conformation.

Polly produced 11 foals, of which all but one were champions in their own right. But the most famous and the most successful foal was Pollyanna which, after a championship career in England, was exported to America and there won many performance classes, becoming the American Champion pony. Today Pollyanna is breeding a line of champions which perpetuate the name of its famous dam, Pretty Polly. Pretty Polly died in 1973, leaving behind a line of ponies which will continue to influence the unique British riding pony.

Below: Richard Meade, who rode Cornishman V at the Mexico Olympics in 1968, shown here on Poacher

Horse shows

THE horse show, which has developed from the old horse fairs, is common to all horse countries, although the content and the methods of judging may–and do–vary considerably. Although sometimes obscured by the entertainment motive, the primary objectives of the horse show is essentially to encourage and improve the production of the breeds and types of horses and ponies and to provide shop-windows for breeders and exhibitors. In a sense, even if a horse show is no more than a show jumping meeting, a frequent occurrence in some European countries where there are, for instance, no hunter classes since the sport does not exist, and no indigenous pony population as in Britain, those objectives are still attained by a test of performance alone. In fact, in countries where horse breeding is largely a state concern selection is, in general, made by this means.

Whilst horse shows embracing most facets of the horse are held in every country, it is probably true to say that they are a far more integral part of the horse scene in the English-speaking countries than elsewhere. There are, however, significant differences in judging methods as well as in the type of classes staged, between those held in Britain and in America. South Africa, Australia and New Zealand tend to follow the British pattern but naturally there are variations imposed by local or national conditions. In Britain horse shows, with the exception of those confined purely to a particular breed or type shown in hand, include jumping competitions and ring events. For some, the showing classes are still the centrepiece of the show, even though their appeal is limited to the more knowledgeable enthusiast. Every show has its classes for ridden hunters, divided by weight-carrying capacity into light, middle and heavyweight, with additional classes for small hunters (15.2 h.h. limit), ladies' hunters (to be ridden side-saddle) and sometimes one for four-year-olds as well. There are also classes for hacks, cobs and for the very numerous riding ponies which are divided by height into three divisions. At the bigger shows there are also classes for working hunters and ponies. As these are judged on the basis of 60 per cent of the marks for performance over a course of fences and 40 per cent for ride, conformation, etc., they give an opportunity to those horses more in the 'handsome-is-as-handsome-does' category who may have collected honourable scars in the hunting field.

The adjudication of the ridden classes boils down to a matter of opinion, the judge's opinion, with which it is possible to agree or disagree but never to argue. In a way these show classes are a sort of equine beauty contest judged on the conformation, action, manners, ride and suitability for their intended purpose of the exhibits, which do not have to prove (except in working classes) their ability to jump. A hunter judge, for instance, is looking for the perfect pattern of a hunter, the sort that will carry a man expeditiously, comfortably and safely across a country throughout a hunting season and remain sound from the opening meet to the closing day. The argument is that if he finds a horse approximating to his ideal of perfection, and much depends on his knowledge and experience, such a horse is ideally equipped to perform his task and any others also, and therefore there is no need for him to prove his ability over a set of fences in a show ring which can in no way resemble the obstacles likely to be met in the open countryside. The judge, in Britain, does however satisfy himself that a horse is as good as it looks by riding every exhibit or at least the top two-thirds of a class, after he has seen them walk, trot, canter and gallop.

Pony classes, which the judge does not ride, do not gallop collectively but exhibitors may gallop their ponies in an individual show. The ponies are judged on confirmation, obedience, good manners and presence.

Hacks are something of a British institution, and though corresponding classes are held elsewhere, none can approach the elegance of a good class of British hacks. They are, of course, judged differently to hunters and are not required to gallop. More emphasis is placed on manners and training in the individual show and once more the British judge rides the exhibits. Essentially this is a riding horse class and one looks for lightness, gaiety, freedom of movement and an indefinable presence.

On the opposite side of the Atlantic horse shows are just as popular. American shows are distinguished by the enormous variety they have to offer in their three distinctive styles of riding: the hunt seat, similar to the British; the stock seat, used for cattle work and its modern ancilliaries and the saddle seat, developed in the Old South and used when showing the walking and gaited horses. A typical American show of from one to twelve days may offer classes for hunters, jumpers, stock horses, trail horses, pleasure horses, walking horses, three- and five-gaited horses, harness horses, roadsters and harness and hackney ponies and there are sure to be equitation classes where riders are judged rather than horses as well as halter classes. Great emphasis is laid on performance with marks awarded for style over fences in hunter classes. The judges *never* ride the exhibits, most of which are under the direction of a professional trainer, which is far from being the case in Britain.

American rules, to an Englishman, seem to be drawn up in such detail as to reduce, insofar as that is ever possible, the expression of an individual opinion. It is not possible, yet, to judge by computer and to remove the element of human fallibility but the American show seems to get as close to that state as it can. What is certain is that without the yardstick provided by the horse show the quality of horses and ponies would go into decline.

David Broome on Beethoven (right), show jumping at Hickstead. The Grey Percheron (left) the most famous of modern draft breeds originated in La Perche, Normandy

Index

Figures in italics refer to illustrations